# BB Remembered

In the churchyard: from *Lepus the Wild Hare*

# BB Remembered

## The Life and Times
## of Denys Watkins-Pitchford

# Tom Quinn

SWAN·HILL
PRESS

First published in the UK in 2006
by Swan Hill Press, an imprint of Quiller Publishing Ltd

**British Library Cataloguing-in-Publication Data**
A catalogue record for this book
is available from the British Library

ISBN 1 904057 82 9
      978 1 904057 82 6

Typeset by Phoenix Typesetting, Auldgirth, Dumfriesshire
Printed in England by St Edmundsbury Press Ltd., Bury St. Edmunds, Suffolk

# Swan Hill Press

An imprint of Quiller Publishing Ltd.
Wykey House, Wykey, Shrewsbury, SY4 1JA
Tel: 01939 261616 Fax: 01939 261606
E-mail: info@quillerbooks.com
Website: www.countrybooksdirect.com

# CONTENTS

# ACKNOWLEDGEMENTS

Thanks to all those who answered my interminable letters; to Mrs Betty Duguid who originally gave me permission to use family photographs and to the BB Society and particularly Bryan Holden. I'm also grateful to Katy, Alex and James for their criticisms and suggestions and to the Trustees of BB's estate. I'd like to thank my friend and fishing companion Richard Smith and the ever helpful Keith McDougall. Finally, thanks to John Beaton and Rob Dixon who so skilfully put the words and pictures together.

Quotations and illustrations are reproduced by permission of BB's agent David Higham Associates and the Trustees of the BB estate: frontispiece and page 13, *Lepus the Wild Hare*, Eyre & Spottiswood 1962; pages 20, 86, *Lord of the Forest*, Methuen 1975; pages 23, 41, 48, 54, 63, 99, *Indian Summer*, Michael Joseph 1984; pages 25, 61, *Brendon Chase*, Hollis and Carter 1947; page 27 *A Child Alone*, Michael Joseph 1978; page 35 *The Pool of the Black Witch*, Methuen 1977; pages 37, 92, *Ramblings of a Sportsman Naturalist*, Michael Joseph, 1979; pages 38, 43, 108, *Confessions of a Carp Fisher*, Eyre & Spottiswood,1950; pages 42, 89, *Fisherman's Folly*, Boydell Press, 1987; pages 56, 59, *Birds of the Lonely Lake*, Benn 1961; page 66, *Wild Lone*, Eyre & Spottiswood, 1938; pages 69, 71, 84, 97, *Little Grey Men*, Eyre & Spottiswood, 1942; page 74 *September Road to Caithness*, Kaye & Ward 1962; page 76, *The White Road Westwards*, Kaye & Ward, 1961; pages 77, 82, 102, *The Autumn Road to the Isles*, Kaye & Ward 1959; page 79, *Bill Badger and the Pirates*, Methuen, 1960; page 91 *The Sportsman's Bedside Book*, Eyre & Spottiswood, 1937; page 100, *The Countryman's Bedside Book*, Eyre & Spottiswood, 1942.

# 1

# INTRODUCTION
# – WHAT WAS HE LIKE?

THE ODDEST thing about BB is that he became a moderately successful writer despite the difficulties raised by deciding to write under a pseudonym chosen not because it made him sound intriguing or mysterious but based on the size of lead shot he used to shoot geese. Even today in the British Library if you type in BB without the inverted commas – ie instead of "BB" – you find that the machine fails to locate a single one of his books. If you type BB in with single inverteds – thus 'BB' you get the same result. In some libraries you may bring up a few of his books if you use the wrong inverted commas or if you inadvertently leave an additional space between even one set of inverteds and the letters themselves.

In short, it's a muddle that cannot have made life easy for the fledgling writer when he sent his first book to the publishers in the late 1930s, but then the world in which BB – or Denys Watkins-Pitchford – lived when that first book was consigned to the village post master was a very different world from the one we inhabit now. I suspect it was a world that simply accepted that a writer might have an odd name. Today no writer starting out on his career would choose a name like BB – in a world where getting anything published is extremely difficult the would-be writer needs a name that sounds glamorous or exotic; that

1

BB in the early 1980s.

catches the public imagination, to use the current jargon.

BB was a man who fitted into the world that was passing away, not the world he survived into. He chose a name he liked and that was as short and pithy as his real name was long and – in his view at least – unmemorably complicated. It was also a name that was central to what was once called sport when sport meant shooting and fishing not football, cricket or any other pastime.

Of course looked at from another point of view BB was as aware as any modern image maker or publicist that some effort has to be made to get the public if not on your side then at least to recall you – BB was at least difficult to forget if only because it was unusual.

The word unusual is probably an apt if rather banal description of BB the man, which is what this book hopes to evoke through the memory of some of his friends and through his own scattered autobiographical references. Like many writers BB included a great deal of autobiographical detail – some thinly disguised some not – in his work. Even his children's stories are in a sense versions of childhood fantasies that held him so tightly in their grip that in old age he felt their meaning more deeply than ever. He seems fervently to have believed that the woods and fields to which he felt so attached had a life of their own and one that was not merely organic. BB's most fervent admirers may be rather offended on behalf of their hero at my description of him in the opening paragraphs of this

Going home: BB at 80 outside Lamport Rectory.

book as a moderately successful writer. By moderately successful of course I meant only in the financial sense, for BB did not make a fortune by writing and those who love his work find it impossible to understand that his reputation is not higher. But from a financial point of view moderately successful is about right – for BB just to be able to live by his pen was an achievement for at times he faced real financial hardship, despite working hard at his writing and at his other great love: painting and drawing.

BB's agent for many years, Jacqueline Korn of David Higham Associates knew him well. She believes that BB's first love – from a work point of view – was always art, but that he found he could tell an engaging story and that he could make a living at it. With a few books under his belt and the knowledge that publishers liked his art work BB gave up the only full time job he ever had – as a schoolmaster – and took the plunge. He tried to live by his pen and though at times it looked as if the experiment might fail he hung on, propelled as much I think by the fact that writing gave him time to return to the woods and fields he'd known as a boy as by any conviction that he could succeed. The fact that he succeeded is not in question and among his admirers there is not a doubt that if he is not to be judged among the great writers he is at least unique. Most of his books may be out of print but they can still be obtained fairly easily and we know, as it were, what they are like. But the real question that prompted the writing of this book is not a question about the books or the artwork. It is a simple question though very difficult to answer. It is: what was BB like?

# 2

# First Meeting

Specialist magazines can be a real bore, but I was lucky. When I landed a job in the editorial office of *Shooting Times and Country Magazine* back in the early 1980s it was still a country magazine – in other words the country magazine part of the title was still important and where shooting magazines now are entirely and only about shooting, the old *ST* as it was affectionately known was still filled each week with a healthy mix of natural history, fishing, anecdotes from the distant past, accounts of country characters – and of course shooting. Today it is filled with far more technical articles on gun cleaning, trigger mechanisms, on techniques for shooting more clay pigeons, more game.

Until the 1980s a succession of talented, whimsical, sometimes eccentric editors had retained the magazine's Victorian virtues of comprehensiveness and quirkiness. And if the contents were eclectic and even eccentric so too were the staff. A famous and very talented editor in the 1960s and 70s didn't shoot at all – in fact he had been a senior officer at the RSPB but he was a great countryman with a ferocious eye for detail and the magazine's circulation rose steadily under him. His predecessor, who had edited the magazine through the 1950s, was a shooting man but also a great eccentric who regularly caught pigeons alive on the office windowsill – *ST* was then still based in Fleet Street – and then hid them under his bowler hat in the street outside. He would then wait to see the look on the first person to kick the hat or pick it up. He was a huge practical joker, heavy drinker and smoker who used to

5

shout regularly that he never trusted a man who didn't drink too much. This neat reversal actually made a lot of sense – Noel Sedgwick believed that when a man was drunk you found out what he was really like because having lost his inhibitions he would no longer be on his best behaviour. Most of the editorial staff, but by no means all, were public school educated but the magazine attracted mavericks who loved the countryside and country sports more than they loved the idea of making money.

The very early 1980s was the last period during which some of the old traditions of the magazine survived – the staff would sometimes disappear at lunchtime to fish or go home. There were people in the office who seemed to come in and do nothing for a few hours before mysteriously vanishing only to re-appear the next day for no apparent reason. Staff snoozed away the years or made occasional attempts to turn the magazine into something modern and more commercial only to be lulled back into the steadier rhythms of the past.

The essentially amateur nature of the magazine wasn't entirely a good thing and hankering after some lost whimsical idyll in publishing is as foolish as hankering after some vanished world in any other commercial sphere. With more magazines on the market and far more competition *Shooting Times* was forced to modernise and that process was completed when it was sold to one of the biggest magazine publishers in the world and it became a hard hitting if rather dull shooting magazine with no extraneous material about the countryside. But BB fitted into the old world of *Shooting Times* perfectly because he was himself a maverick; he was a countryman who loved birds but also loved shooting them and who saw no contradiction in shooting a goose and then, finding he'd only wounded it, taking it home and nursing it back to health so it could become a loved pet and the best guard 'dog' he ever had.

But it was through *ST* that I first met BB. Each fortnight a battered looking typescript would turn up in the stack of post the magazine received each day. Postmarked Thrapston,

6

BB's scraperboards have the quality of fine woodcuts. This is from *Lepus the Wild Hare.*

Northants, and in an old brown envelope that looked like it was part of a stock bought fifty years earlier, the handwriting on the envelope was unmistakable. BB's letters were formed in such a way that they simply could not be mistaken for any one else; his handwriting was small, delicate and linked with loops and half formed letters. In theory it should have been impossible to read. In practice it wasn't difficult at all. But his typing was appalling. Like most good professional writers he always went through his work after he'd typed it and his blue ink squiggles were visible everywhere, but his old typewriter had usually knocked a few holes in paper that looked as if he'd found it in an old dusty cupboard where it had lain undisturbed for more than a century. It was old thick lined paper from what might have been a Victorian ledger and folded many times to squeeze it into a too narrow envelope. But there was a pace and gentleness to the writing that made the sub editors vie with each other to re-type and correct his latest effort. Even at its worst – and at this late stage it was sometimes rather scrappy – his copy read easily and somehow reeked of quiet lanes and bird-filled hedges

In 1985 BB was eighty and I suggested that the magazine should interview him to celebrate the occasion. He was, after all, the magazine's oldest and longest serving contributor, a man who'd known editors back in the 1920s and 30s of whom most of us had never heard. Everyone in the office knew vaguely that BB was a writer known outside the world of country matters. We also knew he was something of an artist but the true extent of his work in art, children's books, conservation and country writing was not really fully appreciated by anyone. We knew about his art because each of his contributions still arrived with a small scraperboard illustration. He'd obviously rattled these off at high speed as they were usually very sketchy and tiny – a far cry from the large masterful scraperboard illustrations with which he'd illustrated his books. But that he still sent them at all bore witness to the fact that he worked hard well into his eighties and hated to short change anyone who'd offered him work

When the day appointed for the interview arrived I set off up the A1 towards Northamptonshire, a county that, despite its

rural beauties is usually overlooked by tourists and others heading further north for the Lake District, the Yorkshire Dales and other more spectacular destinations. BB knew the pleasures of his own county, however, and had rarely left it. On that morning early in 1985 it was easy to see why. Perhaps more than most counties its very unpopularity had left it still rela-

The Round House at Sudborough, BB's last home.

tively unscathed by modern developments. The countryside rolled away ahead of me with small fields, thick belts of woodland, an occasional stream and villages, churches and farms, shadowing doomsday lines as the poet Philip Larkin might have put it.

From the market town of Thrapston I took the road to Sudborough and the Round House where BB had lived for several decades. The house was and is very unusual – clearly several centuries old and perfectly circular it is tucked into a corner flanked by the main road on one side and facing a narrow road into the village on the other. Behind the house at one time was the seemingly endless gloom of Rockingham Forest only fragments of which remain today.

A small ramshackle room with plenty of glass had been tacked on to the house to shield the front door and provide a store for boots and hats and bonsai trees. Having not yet met BB I already realised that he was capable of surprises – many men of BB's generation and class still found it hard to forgive the Japanese for their treatment of prisoners of war but BB, as I later discovered, had a Japanese fan base and was very keen on growing the bonsai trees I saw beautifully trained and tended that first morning at the Round House.

One's tendency is always to expect a man somehow to match his writing and aware that this could be a wildly foolish supposition I half expected a tall vigorous man like a well fed farmer to open the door – ie a man nothing like the gentle creature seemingly evoked by those fortnightly articles. Instead a small – perhaps five feet seven or eight inches at most – rather rotund man answered my knock, smiled a little and asked me in. In fact his manner from the outset perfectly matched the gentle unassuming tone of the articles that had arrived each fortnight in those old brown envelopes.

In the interview that I eventually wrote I said that BB seemed in many ways like one of his characters; he really was a rounded sort of creature, blinking owlishly though thick glasses, the lenses of which seemed none too clean. He wore a thick shirt and dark heavy trousers worn in that old fashioned style that gave the impression they were almost held up around the chest. And he wore a thick brown belt with a large buckle. On other days he wore an ill matched jacket and trousers or an ancient three piece pin-striped suit. The fact that he was always dishevelled was part of his charm. But on that first morning it was difficult to avoid the impression that he modelled himself on some gnome-like woodland creature – that may be rather fanciful but it is certainly true that he did not dress up for the interview and the peculiarly vivid sense of his roundness was confirmed when I later discovered that he was born without collarbones.

BB seemed sprightly, but without the intense vitality for which elderly writers from George Bernard Shaw to Graham Greene are often famous. His was an assured steady presence that did not betray anything decrepit, but it was clear through his thick lensed glasses that his eyes were not as good as they once were and in fact he had already lost the sight in one eye completely. He had what is generally described as a crisp military moustache – his one concession to vanity so far as I could see – and it was something I was later to see in photographs taken of him back in the 1950s and earlier, yet he had nothing of the crisp or military about him in any other sense. He had not lost his hair and he wore it still in the style he'd had as a boy. A neat side parting and cut short.

The Round House itself was untidy but not excessively so and contained a few good old pieces of furniture that he had probably inherited from his parents. The dining room was to the right of the hall and here we had tea with a caged bullfinch for company and his black labrador. BB's daughter Angela sat at one end of the table, BB at the other. Angela ate raw onions while we drank our tea and explained that they were excellent for preventing colds, something with which BB agreed but with a gentle smile that suggested he was not entirely convinced.

After tea BB and I retreated to the sitting room, a room across the hall and opposite the dining room. Here the difficulties of living in a round house were more apparent. Pictures stood out awkwardly on the walls and a long case clock couldn't be made to fit anywhere really happily, but BB loved the house and knew its history. It had been lived in he thought by the toll keeper who guarded the road through the forest – a lovely story that spoke of just the kind of world that BB would have transformed and used in one of his children's stories.

I've described something of the house because it seemed then and during our later meetings to reflect in a rather general way the character of BB – it was straightforward and unfussy, a little unkempt and certainly unmodernised. It had a sort of den like feel to it; never well lit and with small original windows it was the sort of place one would imagine a mole or a badger hiding away.

When we sat and talked he showed me a good copy of a picture by Velasquez he'd made while an art student and there were one or two of his bird paintings, but neither here nor in the dining room were there any books other than his own. Back in the dining room, file copies of his own books were lined up along the top of an old upright piano, but he rarely read other authors and mentioned only Hudson and Jefferies as favourite writers. The interview was one of the most fascinating I'd ever been involved with, not so much for what it revealed as for what it did not.

Politicians, senior businessmen and others at risk of being interviewed by the media are often sent for media training. What this means is that they go somewhere and spend a great deal of money discovering that there is an art to being interviewed. It consists in arriving at the interview knowing exactly what you want to say and saying it regardless of any questions you might happen to be asked. Well, long before such training was available and for very different reasons BB had mastered the art of the interview. He was wonderfully engaging and talkative but he had an unwritten script in his head and somehow managed to stick to it regardless of anything I said. Of course it was only later when I had interviewed BB several times that I realised his story was only a series of variations on a theme. Other interviewers I spoke to while

Lepus again: BB transformed the scraperboard as a medium for book illustration.

researching this book had the same story to tell – BB's life story was something he had by heart and it concealed far more than it revealed. In all my subsequent meetings and interviews with BB – probably more than a dozen in all – I never really got beyond the BB I met on that first occasion. It wasn't that he ever refused to answer a question; he somehow seemed to answer it without really doing so; and the reason was just that BB the private man was very private indeed.

Keith McDougal who knew BB from his, Keith's, earliest years, recalled that no one ever got close to BB's inner emotional life – even Douglas McDougal, Keith's father and one of BB's oldest friends recalled that 'he did not unburden – he kept his personal problems to himself.'

Of course in a memoir like this it would be wildly inappropriate to try to find some dark secret or some inner life of turmoil behind the quiet facade. My own view is that no such dark inner BB existed. He had suffered disasters – famously the death of his son Robin aged eight and the premature death of his wife Cecily – but he suffered these stoically as far as possible and though there is no doubt that he never really escaped the sadness of loss, he was a remarkably self contained and quietly confident man.

His stoicism and inner strength and belief had a great deal to do, I think, with the fact that he was born into the comfortable upper middle class in 1905, almost in the middle of the era of Britain's greatest confidence in itself. The British Empire was assured in its role as the mother country of an Empire the like of which had never been seen in history; the church of England was secure in its place as the established church and there were only barely discernible hints that the old order would soon vanish forever.

# 2

# AN EDWARDIAN
# CHILDHOOD

NYONE who has seen BB's childhood home, the beautiful early eighteenth century rectory at Lamport, will probably assume that his father was a wealthy man. In fact though comfortably off he was by no means wealthy. BB's father was the vicar. He was still paid as a result of a complex system of tithes imposed on the local people in a system barely changed since medieval times. Though the Watkins-Pitchfords were what was termed minor gentry they were gentry nonetheless.

It is hard.today to grasp the enormous power and significance of the world of the 'gentleman' in Edwardian England. To get some idea of the power of the term word consider the following anecdote. When BB was still a child the philosopher Bertrand Russell was chosen above H.G. Wells, the novelist, to be a parliamentary candidate for the simple reason that Russell was a gentleman and Wells a cad. Both men were famous, both had enjoyed the attentions of a string of mistresses, but Russell was the son of an old aristocratic family where Wells was the son of a washerwoman and housekeeper. In Edwardian England birth still counted for far more than achievement. And this seems to have been accepted by all classes. It would have been difficult to find anyone, aside from a few radicals, who did not think that by birth, by their very genetic make up, the children of those who did not work with their hands (or better still did nothing at all) were inherently superior to the

15

Lamport Rectory where BB was born in 1905.

children of lesser mortals. Being the son of a washerwoman was a serious social sin and Wells was rejected because of it. In short he was not a gentleman.

BB, of course, was not born into a family of aristocrats but he was only one level down from that. The confidence of status was to mould BB's personality in such a way that he developed a deep sense of security allied to a firm if modest belief in his own abilities.

His forebears on both sides seem to have been clergymen, lawyers and doctors. For centuries the clergy had tended to be drawn from the younger sons of the gentry. They were gentlemen forced into the church (or the army) because as younger sons could not inherit where they had older male siblings. Because they were gentlemen they had to be found something genteel and reasonably well paid to do. Thus started a tradition from which BB benefitted enormously. The living at Lamport was given to his father because Walter Watkins-Pitchford had been to a university and had been ordained and was a gentleman. The rectory was the second of the two great local houses and therefore suitable for the vicar as a reflection of his status in the area but the Reverend Walter Watkins-Pitchford never owned the house. The family was given the big eighteenth century rectory to live in and a sufficient income to ensure they could employ at least half

Lamport church: BB's father was the rector.

a dozen servants – BB remembered a houseman, cook, three maids, a gardener and a gardener's boy.

From the cook who prepared all the meals to the maid who lit the fires early in the morning, everything was done for the three boys and their parents – BB recalled that if the sitting room fire had died down in the evening his father or mother would ring for the maid to come and throw another log on!

So BB grew up in a secure world where by virtue of his birth and parentage he was deferred to by men and women far older than he was – as a child wandering the gardens he would have accepted as the natural order the fact that the gardener tipped his hat to the child; that the maids curtseyed to his mother and nodded perhaps rather nervously when his father descended from his study. The grandeur of the house can be judged by the fact that, with nine bedrooms a stable block and four big reception rooms it was sold recently for more than £1.5 million.

The fixed order of this world of deference where everyone knew and accepted his or her place gave BB an inner strength, a belief in himself that lasted through later difficulties. It is certain, for example, that in material terms life was never so easy again for BB. After leaving the big house he lived in digs and in a succession of smaller houses and never again (except for one short period soon after his marriage) with servants. To understand what BB was like we have to remember that old saying: give me the child till he is seven and I will give you the man.

BB was essentially an Edwardian. He believed in the established order and had nothing of the radical about him. During the general strike of 1926 for example he would not have dreamed of doing anything other than supporting the establishment – which is why he became a special constable.

At a period when writers and artists particularly, looked forward and experimented with new forms, embracing science and new technology – the machine age – BB looked back to a world of horses and smock-wearing shepherds, to remote fields and abandoned villages. All his books represent in my view a longing for the past but particularly his own rural past. BB's autobiography, *A Child Alone*, reveals the enormous contribution to his character made by the countryside of Northamptonshire as it was when he was a child.

BB never went to school. He was educated at home by a series of governesses, a local schoolmaster, Mr Abbott, and by his father, but in practice this meant that he spent a great deal of time on his own or out wandering the fields and hedgerows. Alone in the wide landscape and happy and secure in the knowledge that a big fire and a secure home awaited him back at Lamport, he was never again to be at one with life in the way he was as a child. The rest of his life was an attempt in painting, drawing and writing to return to what the poet A.E. Housman, in his 'A Shropshire Lad', called the land of lost content.

> Into my heart an air that kills
> From yon far country blows
> What are those blue remembered hills
> What spires what farms are those?
>
> This is the land of lost content
> I see it shining plain
> The happy highways where I went
> And cannot come again.

It is hard to know now whether the fact that BB was a twin had much influence on his life and character. Twins are usually said to have some special bond that lasts through thick and thin. With BB it doesn't seem to have been the case – although he insisted that they were very close there is little evidence for it and having lived together for a while in Essex when they were in their early twenties they parted for more than forty years when Roger emigrated to Canada. When, a few years before he died, Roger returned to live with BB at the Round House, BB treated him gently and with enormous tact as if somehow Roger had been dealt a poor hand in life, but this had more to do with BB's own kindness to a close member of his family.

From *Lord of the Forest*, published in 1975.

BB told me that Roger had become a well-known radio broadcaster in Canada where he spent most of his adult life but that he had experienced a 'disastrous marriage.' Certainly Roger tended to talk endlessly about himself when anyone came to see BB – it wasn't jealously one suspects but rather a feeling of being left out. Whether this dated back to their early days in the Rectory when perhaps they competed for their parents' attention it is hard to say, but BB seems to have led a charmed life as a child precisely because, unlike Roger, he was not sent away to school.

There is no suggestion that he was in any way favoured by their parents, but the fact that BB was considered delicate meant that he was kept away from school, a decision that had enormous consequences both for BB's own developing character and for his relationship with his twin.

The twins were parted early and any closeness BB might have felt to Roger was transferred to the streams and fields, the woods and meadows and all the creatures they contained. BB often said – it was part of that ready made script of his – that as a child he was usually alone but not often lonely, a crucial distinction. I think in some ways Roger suffered more by their parting. Sent away to school among boys he did not know he was probably far more lonely in many ways than the apparently isolated BB who met odd characters, farm workers and fishermen on his ramblings and was always able to return home across the fields to safety and security.

These middle aged and older men would have been young in the later part of the nineteenth century; they remembered the excitement of the early railway; they told tales of huge pike in the local lakes and endless tracts of empty woodland, of remote cottages lit only by oil and of country characters and reclusives. Many of these tales were absorbed by BB and re-cycled in his stories.

BB was born into a world that in many ways now seems unimaginably distant. When he arrived in the world on 25 July 1905, medicine, for example, was rudimentary by today's standards. This may explain why no one had the least idea that his mother was about to give birth to twins. In Edwardian

England and indeed right up until after the Second World War the survival of both twins if they were born naturally was unusual. The least complication meant the death of one if not both infants and sometimes of the mother also. But Denys, as he was later christened, and the surprise second child, Roger, survived. In a way that seems to typify the period and the social status of those involved, grapes were sent by Lady Isham from the great house to celebrate the birth.

Few are still alive who knew BB as a child which is hardly surprising given that he did not achieve the levels of fame that produce widespread record keeping and that he did not go to school. What we know about his earliest years almost all comes from his own account in *A Child Alone* and from interviews he gave over the years.

This remarkable book was a bestseller not just because it appealed to BB's growing number of devotees when it was first published in 1978 but also because it has much in common with BB's children's stories – and indeed with his writing about the countryside.

The book starts with the terror of impending death. BB remembers being in bed in a candle-lit room with terrible stomach pains. This first attack of appendicitis passed after some time but the family was always uneasy that the problem would recur and if it did the results could be fatal. Death by inflammation of the bowels as appendicitis was then known was common in the early years of the twentieth century. But BB was lucky for ether had been discovered a few decades earlier and the need for hygiene during any operation was known. When the disease did recur the decision was made: BB must be operated on before the appendix ruptured.

A large kitchen table was scrubbed, BB's stomach was painted with iodine and he was knocked out with a pad of ether. When he woke a few hours later he had a six inch scar and was presented with a jar containing what he described as a 'large lobworm'– his diseased appendix. The doctors, as it turned out, had been just in time for the appendix was about to burst. What is so interesting about the opening of *A Child*

Squirrel scraperboard from BB's collection of his own work, *Indian Summer*, published in 1984

*Alone* is that it reveals that BB's strongest memory of childhood is the fear of dying. As he says, this fear was tied up more with what he would lose by dying than fear of where he might be going. It seemed so cruel, as he says himself, that having been allowed a short time in a world of wonders he should be whisked out of it. Fishing and shooting, the fun of tramping the fields on endless summer days – how could he bear to lose all this? The wonderful world 'its colours lights and shades' would go on without him – it was unbearable.

Despite the faith of his father in a benign God, BB never seems convinced. As a child and as a man he loved the sheer physicality of the world too much to relish the prospect of some spirit life. Again and again we are told that it is the song of the blackbird, the smell of crushed leaves in wet mud, the sounds of the winter wind under the eaves that he loves, but he loved them for themselves not because they were the creations of a supernatural being. But nature on its own was not enough. BB would have agreed that one is never closer to nature than when in pursuit of it. He had much less of the modern child's sentimentality about animals and birds. He loved birds and he loved to hear their song but he also loved the idea of being a hunter and many of the proudest moments of his childhood are moments when he was able to return to the rectory after a day in the fields with a bag of perch from the ponds or a few rabbits or pigeons. His passion for shooting and fishing can be seen clearly in his own favourite of his children's books: *Brendon Chase*. Here there are detailed accounts of killing rabbits and eating their kidneys and hearts for breakfast – it is difficult to imagine such a book being a bestseller today.

Animals lived and animals died. Butterflies were fascinating but for BB the child and the man they were there to be caught and collected as were wild birds' eggs. It was part of the natural order of things, but for BB there was something more. The woods and fields and the animals that lived in them, along with the houses and churches and farms had a deeper life. Though he was certainly not conventionally religious BB

24

A superb BB cover. *Brendon Chase* was originally published in 1944.

seems to have been highly sensitive to what he would have described as the spirit of things. One of his earliest memories is of being told that when the doctor arrived as his mother went into labour, the maid saw a monkey on the coachman's shoulder. A few years later, aged four, BB saw a crab-apple faced gnome standing between his bed and that of his twin. He and Roger had an imaginary friend called Miss Skulls and once they saw what they called the Peak on the Balcony – a dark shadowy creature that ran along the high parapet at the top of the house. Later in another house BB came across the ghost of an old monk and wherever he fished and shot in later years he had a sense that other long dead sportsmen had left some echo of themselves among the trees and by the waterside.

The fact that BB's birth and that of his twin was without complications may well have had something to do with BB's lack of collarbones – he certainly believed and once said that it meant that apart from his head there was nothing else preventing his arrival. The lack certainly gave him an odd appearance and he was deeply hurt in childhood when his grandmother said: 'My, you are ugly!'

Certainly he was very small, and fair haired like his mother while Roger was taller – a good four inches taller – and dark like their father. BB was cossetted by his mother – perhaps because even before the attack of appendicitis he suffered terribly from colds each winter and from tonsilitis. Removal of his tonsils was to involve a second operation before he was ten. The cossetting irritated him because it interfered with his freedom – his freedom to climb dangerous trees, to make dams across lakes and streams, to disappear for whole days in the remote countryside. In his own mind he was tough and resouceful – he tells us he had a bear-like hug and often put it to good use in fights with his brothers.

BB's mother Edith was tiny – perhaps 4ft 8in – fair and an accomplished violinist. Like her husband she was descended from what might best be termed the solid middle and upper classes: doctors and teachers rather than those who did not have to work at all but lived on their estates and investments. She was was clearly a calm, loving parent and resourceful – when Roger climbed out onto the parapet at the top of the rectory aged about five she stayed calm and coaxed him back in as if he'd just stepped into the wrong part of the room. She had great presence of mind– if she had panicked Roger would have panicked too and could easily have fallen to his death. BB never describes her or his father as particularly affectionate in a physical sense. In a curiously revealing paragraph in *A Child Alone* he describes where his real affections lay – with Nicky, his governess.

> I loved Nicky with all my being for my parents had little to do with us until Nicky went away . . . I used to lie in her lap and snuggle up so my nose was in the hair behind her ear. She had a round freckled face and very lovely soft brown eyes. I always promised I would marry her when I was big enough . . . When Nicky went on her annual holiday I cried for days . . .

BB's father was a more distant figure and in BB's own words he was a typically remote Edwardian patriarch, though in later life he grew more gentle and thoughtful particularly in the last years before his death in 1944. When BB was a child his parents called him Tuppeny after a range of small rubber toys popular at the time that cost tuppence each. His father was stern but artistic and musical – BB complains that he was usually too busy to play with him because he spent all his time at the piano composing. Intriguingly, though I can find no trace of them, Walter Watkins-Pitchford wrote at least two operas that were broadcast by the BBC. As a student at Trinity College Dublin he entered a poetry competition and, so the legend goes, beat George Bernard Shaw who had also entered – I suspect that this may be an apocryphal tale for Shaw left Ireland in 1876, never attended the university and wrote novels early in his career.

But BB's father seems to have been more of an influence than BB's mother. BB tells us that his father was a stern disciplinarian who beat his three sons now and then with a cane. BB insisted it did no harm and that it was far better than the 'mollycoddling' that today produces young hooligans – a view expressed with some vehemence in *A Child Alone*. His father was also 'like Mr Toad in the *Wind in the Willows*' always full of new schemes and enthusiasms – for cars, disastrous central heating systems, morris dancing, radios, steam baths and motorbikes. Walter Watkins-Pitchford had no interest of any kind in natural history or sport, the enthusiasms that pushed BB out into the wider world away from the house during the long days when his two brothers were away at prep school in Scotland.

Throughout *A Child Alone* we are constantly made aware of the rigid class system that was maintained in Edwardian England. BB and his brothers, being the sons of a gentleman, were invited to theatricals and parties attended by 'the county families' – that is by the families of the gentry. The sons of the farm labourers and shopkeepers were never invited. But BB seems to have found real companionship not with these well-born youngsters but rather with much older, working men. Had these men been children the association would have been banned – the children of the minor gentry did not play with working class children – but somehow the gardener, the coachman, the postman and the smith could take the young gentleman fishing or shooting without breaking the social distinctions.

Thus it was that BB's earliest memories are filled not just with the woods and fields where he found his entertainment but also with the older men who worked for his father or lived in tiny cottages round about and worked on the farms or for other well off families.

Butterflies from *Indian Summer*.

In *A Child Alone* BB seems eager to repay some kind of debt to these men and again and again he tells us that they worked long hours for 'a pittance'; but whatever their status in the world there was something magical about them to a young boy and they became the friends of his most impressionable years. In one or two cases long after they had departed or retired BB tried to track them down to thank them for all that they had done.

There was Old Gunn the gardener, Yerry his successor, Will Hedge the carpenter, the postman Bob Dickens and old Job Perkins with whom BB went fishing to Scaldwell Pond.

One of the curious things about BB's own memories of his childhood and young adulthood is that they reflect exactly the view of the world he had in his eighties. Many of the views he attributes to his young self echo the quotation he used at the front of all his books:

> The wonder of the world, the beauty and the power, the
> shapes of things, their colours, lights and shades; these
> I saw. Look ye also while life lasts.

This was a quotation he clearly didn't know until much later – and again it is as if, for the purposes of his autobiography, he has selected those parts of his childhood that fit the image of himself he wished to maintain as an adult: the young hunter passionately fond of the countryside, natural history, fishing and shooting; the young naturalist with a rare, almost spiritual link to the fields and woods of a vanished England.

It has been said that the dominant cultural tone of the Edwardian era in England is one of melancholy longing. It was a longing for the past that was to weave a curious romance around, for example, the Great War. It explains why even before the worst slaughter and waste of that conflict was known the war was being memorialised in a unique way that still affects us. The idea of a lost generation seems far more real when applied to the First World War compared to the Second, despite the fact that far more human beings were killed in the Second World War.

Like many English artists and writers in the early part of the twentieth century, BB was affected greatly by this deeply rooted longing for the past. He captured and continued to capture for the rest of his life a sense of England's glory passing; of the destruction of a world of social certainties and rural beauty; for BB what was passing was the perfection of a countryside still undamaged by the motorcar and 'terrible pesticides'. The tone is the tone of his contemporaries or near contemporaries Elgar, A.E.Housman and John Betjeman – it's a lament for the past that is still hugely compelling for us even today.

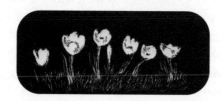

Apart from the sounds and scents of the countryside which affected BB from such an early age, fishing was his first love. And when he writes about the number of ponds and un-polluted streams within just a few miles of his home he is pointing up a genuine change in the countryside because intensive farming had not got underway in the early part of the twentieth century. The desire to make as much money as possible out of every acre had not yet led to the grubbing up of hedgerows and the filling in of ponds – something that happened in a widespread and systematic way as the century progressed. In 1912 when BB was seven – and about the time he would have made his first fishing forays – odd corners of fields were still often left uncultivated; old ponds were kept to wash the carthorses' feet (it prevented them getting farsy – a kind of foot rot) or left in peace simply because they had been there as long as anyone could remember, and the hedges were allowed to grow up rather than be flailed every year and made to look like surburban privet. There were more people about in the countryside too, with an average of one man on the land for every acre – a century later that figure was down to one man per one hundred acres. Villagers lived and worked in the same area, many travelling no more than a few dozen miles in any direction at any time in their lives.

The downside of this rural idyll, which BB only occasionally recognises, is that the countryside was unspoiled partly at least because most local people were poor. The coming machine age of cars and pesticides, tractors and combines which destroyed the hedges and ponds, the remote fields and cart tracks did at least change one thing for the better: it made a much higher standard of living available to far more people.

For the gentry – even the minor gentry – the period before the First World War was the last golden age. By the 1920s swingeing taxes and death duties led to the abandonment of many big houses and by 1956 it is estimated that one big country house a day was being demolished. During this period once remote hamlets and villages became busier as roads were widened and tarmaced over; bigger trunk roads were built and the former dominance of the railway began to decline.

How extraordinary it seems now that BB could write of Faxton, an outlying village that his father served on Sundays:

> As the years went by more and more houses (in Faxton) fell into ruin and families grew less and less and finally, after my father's death, the church was pulled down stone by stone, the elms were blown down by winter gales and when I last visited it only the stone altar remained, half hidden by nettles . . . I had the feeling that nothing was permanent – pictures, sensations, sounds, passed before me like some panorama.

Faxton was an extraordinary village for many reasons but chiefly because there was no road to it – if you lived there you had to reach your cottage or the church on foot across the fields.

The whole process of these changes in the countryside happened during BB's lifetime and his stories – whether children's books or his books about shooting, fishing or the countryside in general – reflect the longing he felt for the countryside of his childhood and for his childhood itself.

# 4

# WITH ROD AND LINE

As a child BB spent his summers wandering about searching for various new places to fish but he had his favourites where, for example, the small perch – which he took home to eat – would bite almost endlessly and the deeper lake where a 2lb roach once came and took his bait.

> One early summer morning I slipped out of the house with some bread paste mixed with honey and fished a new place under a hawthorn where the water was no more than three feet deep...I had never fished before in the early morning and the novelty of it led to a new enchantment with its minted freshness and singing birds. I cast out my honeyed bait. Before long my heart beat fast for out from the lily thickets came cruising a shoal of the big roach we could never catch...I saw one monster come gliding up and make a round mouth at my bread paste ball. I struck and landed a wonderful silver prize which was near the two pound mark. Incidents like this made my loneliness more bearable.

There is a contradiction in much of this — when BB rode Little Man, the Shetland pony he borrowed from a neighbour, he describes riding out alone but that he 'preferred it that way'. He frequently tells us too that he was alone but not lonely; yet on several occasions in *A Child Alone* he also confesses – as in the extract above – that he dreaded the day when his brothers would be left at the station to return to school and that it was

Fishing produced some of BB's finest scraperboards. This is from *The Pool of the Black Witch* (1974).

only moments spent fishing when, as in the case of that 2lb roach, he landed a big fish that made his loneliness more bearable.

In some way like most of us BB wanted it both ways; he loved the freedom of being alone. He could choose to fish where he liked and ride wherever the fancy took him but occasionally realised that fishing with a companion was far more fun – catching a big fish alone means there is no one to share your joy and sense of achievement. There is no one to discuss odd sights and sounds or the weather. BB's writing is filled with a longing for solitude but this was a solitude that often fed his melancholy streak.

The pleasures of fishing reached their apogee in outings with BB's great friend Job Perkins. Perkins, who had come back from the Great War unscathed, would have been at least twenty years older than BB and though we can be sure that he was suitably deferential to the young master from the big house, they did share a great love of sport. BB's descriptions of Perkins' fishing tackle – a huge stiff bamboo pole and a reel made by the local blacksmith that weighed at least three pounds – are wonderfully evocative. When Perkins' big white homemade float began to slide away – indicating a pike had taken the bait – he would whisper to BB, 'Watch me whip im!'

If the monster pike turned out to be a small one the power of Perkins' strike with the massive rod would sometimes propel the poor fish into the air and it would land with a thump behind them.

BB's love of fishing never left him and in the last years of his life he was driven regularly by a friend to local stillwaters where he would fish for trout from a boat. What makes BB's attitude to fishing and his writing about it so compelling is the fact that he cared so little for the technical aspects of the sport. In a magazine article he wrote towards the end of his life he claimed he only ever used half a dozen flies and he had little interest in the latest wizard gadgetry. And in his great fishing book *Confessions of a Carp Fisher* he is at some pains to point out that the book is not a treatise on how to catch more carp; the

The mystery of ancient ponds is perfectly captured in this illustration
from *Ramblings of a Sportsman Naturalist*.

BB's own design for the jacket.

book's magic lies in the fact that rather than explaining how to catch carp it explains why they are so difficult to catch.

The old fashioned romantic in BB always liked to emphasise the mystery of things – the remote forgotten nature of an old house or farm; the long forgotten depths of an old pike lake unfished for decades. In the case of the carp the emphasis was on the mystery of the fish, its habits and way of life. If you only read *Confessions* and wanted to try carp fishing for the first time you would very likely never bother – to judge by BB's description of carp fishing the capture of a single fish has something of the miraculous about it.

The real magic of *Confessions of a Carp Fisher* is that it has survived a revolution in fishing techniques that has eliminated the very thing that BB was writing about – modern carp fishing techniques have destroyed a great deal of the mystery of carp fishing and it is this mystery that BB so beautifully evokes.

When *Confessions* was first published in 1950 the record carp stood at about 26lb and as BB says very few fishermen had caught or even seen carp weighing more than ten pounds. Five pounders were so uncommon that they were frequently sent to taxidermists to be set up. Today a five pounder is a tiddler.

Improvements in fishing tackle – particularly the introduction of nylon monofilament along with fixed spool reels that held huge amounts of line and enabled the fisherman to cast long distances – did a great deal in the 1970s and 80s to put an end to the idea that very large carp were uncatchable. Indeed thirty pound fish are now commonly captured and the record fish is well over fifty pounds.

Despite the loss of the mystery surrounding the fish BB's book is still hugely popular – it's a classic, not of instructional literature, but of the atmosphere, the sights and sounds of fishing. For BB the magic of carp fishing was identical to the magic of any other kind of fishing. It had to do with mysterious ponds and forgotten lakes hidden away in odd corners of the countryside. It had to do with a band of often lonely seeming men who spent weeks at the waterside growing ever more unkempt, their eyes steadily taking on a glassy hue, almost like the men who returned shell shocked from the Great War. As BB himself wrote:

> Carp fishing is a most curious form of fishing and calls for a very special turn of mind and character. First there is the quality of patience… your habitual carp fisher is a man of inexhaustible patience, no angler born has more than he, not even a wild eyed heron has greater patience and, I may add, watchfulness. He is a man of summer, for the carp is a summer fish. Carp fishers disappear in autumn and are not seen until the following midsummer, nobody quite knows what they do or where they go.

Clearly this is just fanciful (if rather lovely) nonsense: we do know where carp fishers go in winter. They simply stay at home or play golf or do the gardening but when BB tells us they vanish like this it gives them a splendid aura of mystery identical with the mystery of the fish they pursue. BB's desire to conjure a world where hunter and hunted are brought together in the universal mystery of nature is a thread that runs through all his work and it remained consistent throughout his life. Almost out of the blue – it is one of those rare outbursts of feeling in *A Child Alone* – he says it disgusts him that humans refuse to see themselves as animals but the idea that humans are really only animals goes against the Christian concept of what it means to be human; a concept that would have been central to BB's father's firm faith in a Christian God. BB believed in nature and man's part in it but man had the huge added advantage that he could wonder at the world; he could enjoy uniquely the colours, lights and sounds, the pleasures of field and stream, hedgerow and woodland.

If looking back and conjuring an idyllic golden time is central to BB's life and work then *Confessions* is a fine example of the technique and habit of mind in action. It opens with quotes from H.T.Sheringham, a Victorian fishing writer whom BB blames for making him a carp addict. He also quotes at

The contemplative art: from *Indian Summer*.

length the story of the 26lb carp caught by Albert Buckley in 1930 which was the record until Richard Walker, a friend of BB's, and much more of a scientific angler, caught his 44lb record fish in 1952. The effect is to enhance the idea of dedicated men spending months and years in pursuit of leaviathans that would prove too terrifying for ordinary mortals.

The mystery of water whether it contains giant carp or not has always captivated man and not just anglers. Water, the source of life, is eternally compelling for BB who wrote in *Fisherman's Folly*, an odd book originally published as *Be Quiet and Go A Angling*:

> Standing on the old stone bridge the other day and looking over at the brown stream where the minnow shoals were spawning. I began to think about this little stream, how it has run down the centuries, way back into the mists of time. Trees die, as does all life, but this bright water runs eternally, truly as old as the hills.

For BB being at the waterside where there might be a chance to make the aquaintance of another interesting angler was always part of the pleasure. He also delighted in shadowy figures, fishermen who had somehow left their ghosts by the water's edge; he loved strange happenings and inexplicable shadows. He describes, for example, a visit to Beechmere, a mysterious lake he loved to fish, but one that had hardly been fished by anyone for years:

> Save one or two locals – the postman and an old Catholic priest named Father Angelus. Father Angelus in shovel hat and cassock haunted Beechmere for many years. He used to go in the very early summer mornings before other folk were astir and heaven knows what thrills he had in that shadowed place where the wood piegon cooed among the beeches. Year after year he came so the postman said. He stayed

Father Angelus whose story features in *Fisherman's Folly*.

in the neighbouring village, coming round about midsummer day and remaining until early August ... and then there came a year when Father Angelus failed to put in an appearance. He has not been seen since. He has vanished like a migratory fish-eating bird of sombre plumage; there is no one now to wonder where he is, or how he does, or whether, like all living things, he has passed from this world. Yet – laugh if you will at my fancy – whenever I tread that winding path under the beeches at that rare hour when the world is hushed and dim, I think that any moment, at any turn of the way, I shall see him before me, tall and black in his medieval habit, burdened with basket and rod and moving with noiseless tread towards his special pitch.

BB loves this kind of thing – the countryside, the ghost of some vanished angler, the hint of his presence still along the path. Part of his writing seeks a sort of archaic diction too – he 'embaskets' his fish and tells us that 'I remarked, also, a grebe'. This habit of self conscious archaism can be found throughout his children's fiction – in *Brendon Chase* he tells us that the schoolboys 'each at his appointed hour, would embark and entrain for that ancient seat of learning set among the elms ...'

The sense of the past as a special place where things were very different is enhanced by this deliberate use of what sound like old fashioned phrases. Seen from the perspective of the 1970s the life described in *A Child Alone* must have seemed idyllic indeed but BB is looking back with rose tinted spectacles to a time before the disasters that he later suffered – the loss of his only son and of his wife. He is evoking a haphazard series of memories that seem all the more wonderful when seen through the perspective of later upset and disappointment. Again his theme is the land of lost content.

# 5

# AN ARTIST'S EYE

W E NEVER really know why BB began to paint and draw as a child. Certainly he did so and his earliest drawings were clearly praised by his parents. The huge possibilities of art were revealed when he sold – aged just seven – a drawing for a shilling. Having never been to school he was taught by his father as he tells us in *A Child Alone*. He was taught French, Latin and mathematics but clearly excelled at none of these. Later lessons with Mr Abbott in the village produced no better results.

Neither BB nor his brother Roger aspired to go to university which might seem odd given that their father had studied at Trinity College in Dublin and was clearly of an academic turn of mind. In terms of their careers, the boys seem to have been influenced hardly at all by him – Roger found work in a bank which he hated and then worked in horticulture before leaving for Canada and BB left for Northampton Art College at the age of fifteen. 'Each morning I walked the mile to the station to catch the 9.05 train carrying a small hand case which carried my pencils, brushes and paints.'

BB was not an intellectual. He spoke no other language and had few interests outside art, the countryside and field-sports. Apart from one reference to Van Dyke and one to Michaelangelo in *A Child Alone* we get no sense that BB had much interest in art generally at all – he was interested in portraying the countryside and that was it. He owned no art books and did not keep up with modern art at all – he admired Tunnicliffe with whom he had studied for some time in

45

London because, like BB, Tunnicliffe drew and painted animals and birds.

As BB's passion for drawing and painting grew it must have seemed natural to him to draw the things he loved best – animals and birds, fields and meadows, fishermen and carters.

But even as his passion for art grew the first great shock of what must otherwise have seemed a charmed life took place. His elder brother Engel, aged thirteen, returned to school but after a few weeks his parents were summoned and they disappeared mysteriously out of BB's life for a few days. When they returned they took BB and Roger to one side and explained that Engel would not be coming home again and that he had gone to heaven. BB tells the tale in an emotionless way but it is hard to believe that he was not deeply upset by the news.

One of the most haunting parts of *A Child Alone* concerns this death and the later death of BB's own son, Robin. These deaths are linked to the ghosts of the past. When BB's father visited Jerusalem in the early 1900s, as Edwardian clergymen were inclined to do, he met a beggar who asked for alms. Walter Watkins-Pitchford ignored the request and was roundly cursed by the old beggar. A guide explained that the old man had said that the clergyman's eldest son would die along with the eldest son of his second son – which is precisely what happened. BB neither dismisses this as superstitious nonsense nor seems fully to believe it, but he is clearly made uneasy by what looks on the face of it like the working out of the prophecy. For someone who had a great sense of the world as a place full of spirits and ghosts BB was never able fully to dismiss the curse as a piece of mumbo jumbo.

With Engel gone and his father cooped up mostly in his study at the piano BB continued to play about the fields on long summer days and to draw and paint in the evenings by the fire in those far off pre radio and television days. The decision to send him each day to Northampton Art school made sense as, like Roger, he had not inherited or developed his parents' love of music, languages and the arts.

It must have been enormously difficult for BB on that first day at art school. He tells us that he simply stood just inside the door when he arrived and said nothing, having no idea where to go or what to do. Having spent years in the company of the family, servants and local – mostly adult – characters he was suddenly propelled into a world for which he'd had no chance to prepare. He tells us:

> I could not go on sitting at home, gossiping with Perkins, riding about the fields, rambling with my gun, and fishing for pike in the fish pools. It was a sort of Richard Jefferies existence and it led nowhere.

But art school was a shock:

> Due to my sheltered and narrow existence I was painfully shy, even entering a shop was an ordeal. And my first morning at the art school – then at the top of Abingdon Street – was typical. With great trepidation I entered the classroom and instead of going up to the art master – a little man called Rutter who was an excellent teacher and artist – and announcing myself as a new student I stood inside the door, case in hand, not knowing what to do. All the class stared at me while Mr Rutter was busy at the other end of the room.

This initial awkwardness was quickly cleared up and BB's natural confidence meant that within a few days he felt comfortable, but in a way that seems to have typified all his friendships. He was quickly drawn to a like-minded student. 'Most of the students were female. I quickly made friends with a boy called Harding who, like me, was interested in birds and later he came on nesting expeditions to Naseby Reservoir in search of sedge warblers and grebes.'

BB was always modest about his artistic and storytelling talents: 'I had two gifts – an ability to write after a fashion and to paint and draw with a modest degree of skill'. But he had a

Patient heron: from *Indian Summer*.

good eye and an even better hand, carrying off several prizes during his time at the Northampton School of Art. But he found the rather dry academic approach – which included drawing from the antique – irksome and longed to be able to draw from the life. He did eventually move on to life drawing but as he wryly observes in *A Child Alone* the Northampton city fathers would not allow naked or even topless models. His disappointment though unstated is clear!

BB readily admits that he never fully mastered the art of painting in oils – anyone who has seen any of his early pictures of birds will no doubt disagree but BB knew his limitations and the oils have nothing of the original and distinct beauty of his best scraperboards. Indeed it can be fairly said that not only was BB a master in this medium but he really did create the scraperboard as an original medium for book illustration. Before BB came along, as he tells us himself, scraperboard had been used for advertising but even then only rarely. He was the first to see its wonderfully vivid qualities.

Away from mainstream developments in art where Continental and some English artists in the early part of the twentieth century looked to Africa and Asia rather than to the past for their inspiration, there has been a steady and continuous thread of conservatism runing through English art. These conservative artists would have agreed with Sir Alfred Munnings the great horse painter who stood up at the Royal Academy in London and berated artists who refused to paint a tree so that it actually looked like a tree. Of course he was trying hopelessly to hold back the tide of history but his was a view with which BB would wholeheartedly have agreed. Growing up in the English Midlands he would have known little or nothing of the sensation caused by the First Post Impressionist Exhibition held in London in 1910 and followed up some years later by a similarly outrageous show.

The writer and artist Quentin Bell who knew Roger Fry, the organiser of that first exhibition, recalled that there were scenes of violence when the British public was first exposed to what were seen as dreadful daubs by artists such as Cezanne.

'Umbrellas were even brandished,' to use Quentin Bell's memorable phrase.

But for BB it is as if the modern movement had never happened. Bewildered by the modern world that seemed to take him further and further away from the rich rural imagery of his childhood, BB was similarly bewildered by an artistic development that cared nothing for representational art. Representational art was everything to BB. He painted and drew fish and fishermen, horses and carts, deer, rabbits, hares, birds and landscapes and all with as much of the magic and mystery of childhood memories as he could muster.

During his time at the Northampton School of Art BB won a travelling scholarship to Paris – in interviews he always said he couldn't really remember how long he'd spent in Paris but it was probably about three months. He worked in a studio in Montparnasse and attended drawing classes which included naked models – he was both astonished at this development and delighted. To the end of his life he thought shame and embarrassment about the human body ridiculous.

No one seems quite sure where he studied in Paris – it may have been Colarossi's or Julian's where Rothenstein (later to teach BB at the Royal College) had studied or possibly even Carmen's, a school that Whistler had opened in the 1890s.

BB spent a great deal of time in the Louvre copying old masters and tells us that, despite his usual problem with shyness, he quickly found his way around the city. This was probably in the spring and early summer of 1924 for towards the end of that year he was back in Northampton. In the autumn he set off for London and the Royal College of Art. By now the shy boy who had stood at the back of the Northampton School Art room was a far more confident creature. He says himself that even Paris had held no terrors for him after a short while. 'Surprisingly for one who had had such a sheltered upbringing I soon began to find my feet and lost much of my shyness. I was able to travel around Paris without difficulty.'

London was much the same despite initial awkwardness – he arrived late one dark autumn evening at lodgings organised by his parents. They had chosen his accommodation in typical Edwardian fashion with the prime aim of ensuring he didn't fall into bad company – their choice of a vicar as landlord did not inspire BB, however, particularly as he smelled continually of incense and left BB waiting outside in the cold for two hours having forgotten that his new paying guest was due to arrive that day.

The Royal College of Art was based at this time in the Victoria and Albert Museum at the South Kensington end of Exhibition Road. The students had their own, separate entrance and had to sign in and out each day. William Rothenstein (1872-1935) was then principal of the College and though he is generally regarded as a fine artist and is remembered as an excellent teacher BB was rather in awe of him.

On BB's first day while he was drawing a still life of an orange and a book, Rothenstein suddenly appeared out of nowhere, sat next to him and asked if he could estimate the line of the angle between the book and the table on which it was standing. BB had to admit that he hadn't a clue. Rothenstein stalked off without a word and BB ruefully admitted that he had established his reputation as a 'nit wit'.

But he admired his other teachers – he describes how Monnington helped him draw an arm by quickly sketching to the side of the piece on which BB was working: 'The finished work made my effort seem like that of a child of ten. He worked in the style of Da Vinci – fine slanted lines of shade and with a very precise grasp of form.'

This is one of a few memories in *A Child Alone* that doesn't seem to add up. The incident almost certainly happened but BB may well be misremembering some of the details. He appears to be talking about Walter Thomas Monnington (1902–76) but Monnington didn't start teaching drawing at the Royal Schools until 1930, after BB had left.

Having gone through the drawing class BB was at last allowed to paint from the life using colour. He found this extremely difficult though he admits that Rothenstein praised his efforts on a number of occasions.

Once a week he set off for the National Gallery for copying day. He made a copy which he kept by him for the rest of his life, of Velasquez's Philip the Fourth. When he tells us about his art school days there are a few hints about his artistic taste – he tells us that he admired Rothenstein's drawing but thought his portraits woolly compared to the work of the most fashionable, but now less highly regarded, painter of the day, Augustus John whom BB clearly admires. This view hadn't changed when in the 1950s he wrote to Ronald Clough (a friend with whom BB kept up a regular if intermittent correspondence) saying John was the greatest living artist – Picasso was by contrast he said 'The king who had no clothes . . .'

John, considered virtually a genius in his youth – he was described as the English Leonardo – was left behind when the traditional skills of draughtsmanship were overtaken in the twentieth century by the modern movement and its rejection of academic drawing and painting. But like John, BB, along with his fellow students Tunnicliffe and Edward Le Bas was at least (as BB himself said) to achieve the accolade of an entry in *Who's Who*. BB said that a teacher at the Royal School once told him that though he might not ever be a great painter he would always be able to earn a living as an illustrator. That may sound unkind (typically modest, BB didn't think so) but it was a remarkably prescient judgement, for BB was indeed always able to fall back on selling his artwork when times were hard. Right up to the end of his life when his sight was failing he would offer to paint people's dogs and horses and he always had a box of his scraperboards to hand and offered visitors the chance to buy them at £10 a throw. The local auctioneer, in Thrapston, frequently received oils sketches from BB for immediate sale – the joke was that they were often still wet when they arrived!

But if money was never a major consideration for BB – and it was not – the fields and woods and the creatures that lived in them were always at the forefront of his mind. He once said that wherever he was he always felt the steady pull of the fields

52

and woods of Northamptonshire. He never seems to have tired of them.

In London he drew birds and animals when not in the formal classes held each day at college and as that first summer term began to draw to a close he wrote:

> I began to feel an almost irresistible longing for the fields and woods and home – away from the noise of London and its smells. But the term dragged on. As I walked in the early mornings along Exhibition Road to the college I could sense the promise of a perfect summer's day – the plane trees, as yet fresh and green, the layers of their leaves unstirred by the breeze, the pigeons circling and clapping round the courtyard of the Victoria and Albert, the dreamy splashing sound of the fountain.

Eighty years on the courtyard BB knew is largely unchanged – an occasionally gloomy space with the high red walls of the museum shutting out most of the light except on the brightest days. Exhibition Road is far more altered but BB would still recognise many of the buildings. The suburbs of London where BB lodged have, by contrast, changed out of all recognition.

BB had tired of his lodgings with the vicar by the end of his first term and it happened that his twin Roger, having tired of his first job at the bank, had come to London to work with Amos Perry the nurseryman, at Enfield. BB jumped at the chance to move out of central London with its smoke and fogs to what was then still green countryside.

> With considerable gratitude he and I moved to digs in a farmhouse called Chaselands near Gordon Hill. This old house disappeared long ago under a rash of new building. In those days, it was out in the country. From our bedroom window we could look out over green fields with the railway in the distance. On the wall of

our bedroom we hung the stuffed trout from the Blythe Brook and my artistic efforts.

The air of nostalgia is there in this memory of what BB admits was one of the happiest times in his life, a time when he felt close to Roger.

The stark beauty of winter: from *Indian Summer*.

Roger and I were devoted to each other and rarely quarelled and that bond remains. We went on long expeditions at the weekends in summer when we would get old Mrs Wilson to pack us up some sandwiches. We would wander off in the green countryside exploring streams and woods and finding from time to time uncommon nests such as red-backed shrikes. There are no red-backed shrikes at Gordon Hill now – nor anywhere else for that matter.

During the summer vacations back at home BB continued to fish and shoot just as he had done as a boy – and he was still returning home regularly long after he started work as a schoolmaster. Later in life he fished more widely on Fenland canals, carp waters in Devon and Shropshire (including sessions on the most famous of all carp pools, Redmire). He also fished for trout in Scotland and the north of England, and he fished on some of the most famous (and expensive) of the southern chalkstreams but none seem to have worked their way into his soul quite as the waters of Northamptonshire had done.

Nostalgia for his Northamptonshire youth colours a vast amount of BB's writing about the countryside but especially about fishing and the intensity of that nostalgia increased as he grew older. In *Fisherman's Folly*, published in 1987, he emphasises the sense of looking back by adopting a curious pseudo Izaak Walton style to describe a trout fishing incident:

That was a good cast. The worm, a fresh one just put on, landed up in the swift water just as I had wanted it to. I can feel the gentle 'scurr' of the single shot knocking on the stones as the bait is hurried down towards us. The fish (if fish is there) will have his back to us for he will be facing upstream.

I have him by the Venerable Izaak, I have him! And it is no brown trout but a herling; and a good herling at that . . . steady, now he's taking me up the burn. See he

leaps once, twice, thrice – two pounds if he's an ounce.
A murrain on him! Plague take him! He's off!

The magic of fishing clearly has a great deal to do with BB's
own past and the past of fishing itself. Even in the last few

BB illustrated many books by other authors: this is from *Birds of the
Lonely Lake* by A. Windsor Richards and published in 1961.

months of his life he fished occasionally – but now on the wide reservoirs of the Midlands; reservoirs that did not even exist when he was a boy.

Looking back also occasionally tempered the religious scepticism expressed in *A Child Alone* and BB has a more sympathetic view of his father's more orthodox views. BB often said that despite everything the Reverend Walter Watkins-Pitchford was a 'wise old bird.' And in 1949 he wrote:

> But the sun has gone at last, a wind stirs among the oak tops, ruffling the skin of cold clear water. We are all of us waiting, waiting, and the sun and season is in no hurry. It is time to look over my rods, to look to my lines and reels.
>
> We are all of us waiting and I, being an angler, am used to waiting. The peacock butterfly, the tight closed buds, the roots of the meadow grasses are all waiting God's good time. The chiff-chaff which I shall so surely hear is at this moment no doubt hopping in an orange grove in the sun of Spain, the gentle turtle doves are busy in an African jungle. But soon there will come to them uneasy restless thoughts, and perhaps, who knows? – into their diminutive craniums, so delicately wrought, will steal a vision of a little green wood, set in a pleasant meadow, a still dark pool where fish lie basking, the very place where they themselves first entered into this lovely life and where sometimes an idle man sits and fishes and gives thanks to God.

Some may see this as a rather overblown passage – itself an example of *Fisherman's Folly* and expressed in excessively purple prose; yet there seems to be real feeling here. That vision of the wood, the meadow and the still dark pool was not just a vision of the places to which the birds returned; it was a vision of the places to which BB always himself returned.

# 6

# In The Schoolroom

I T HAS BEEN said – with how much truth it is difficult to say – that all fiction is disguised autobiography. In BB's case that disguise is either very thin or non existent. Indeed in one interview BB argued that the greatest children's fiction came from those authors who had themselves lived particularly intensely as a children. BB's own favourite among his own novels, *Brendon Chase*, is an exact fantasy of his own childhood; every day as he was growing up in that remote vicarage he escaped to the woods but of course he always had to return at evening. For Robin, the central character in *Brendon Chase*, there was no need to return home; he and his brothers had escaped to the greenwood.

Early on in the book, Robin tells us about his favourite reading: when he escapes to Brendon Chase he takes with him Thoreau's *Life in the Woods*, *The Amateur Poacher* and *Bevis* by Richard Jefferies. All were favourites of BB's own childhood.

In the child's fantasy the ultimate pleasure would be to escape not just for a day but for ever and live self sufficient among the animals and plants in which man had his natural and happiest place.

Man's natural place was certainly not in an office – as BB's twin Roger discovered – nor in a schoolroom. But like so many young people then and now the daunting day at last came round for BB when, his art school days over, he had to find something to do. Somehow by now – the late 1920s – the old world of which BB might once have hoped to be a part, had vanished. Fifty or even thirty years earlier BB might have followed his father into the church, but by the late 1920s the tithe system was breaking down, the landed interest for the first time was expected to pay taxes commensurate with their wealth and big houses like the rectory at Lamport were soon to be sold and cease to be in the gift of grand local families.

Of course BB would never have fitted into the church

Heron mobbed by crows from *Birds of the Lonely Lake*.

anyway. If he had any faith – and there is evidence, as we've seen, that he did not, at least at this time – it was more in the power of nature than in the established church. Other traditional avenues even supposing he'd wish to take them were also closing: the Army had long taken young men from BB's class as had the Indian Civil Service. Neither would have provided a congenial atmosphere for BB.

Like so many young men of his generation and background – including writers like George Orwell, Evelyn Waugh and Graham Greene – BB decided to become a schoolmaster. He was never enthusiastic about the decision but regarded it as a necessary evil. He had to do something and what else was there?

After a last summer shooting and fishing – including a first trip to the Wash in search of geese – the question of earning an income became, as BB himself said 'paramount'. He had been living on a small allowance provided by his parents (who of course in those pre-grant days had paid for his years through art school) but Roger was earning a living and the pressure was on. BB must have been a rather comical sight when, through the suggestion of a friend of his brother's, he was interviewed for a teaching job in Enfield near where the brothers lodged.

He arrived wearing a bowler hat and was mistaken for the school inspector. Having found the interview room all went well and he was offered the job which he promptly turned down. He then went for an interview to a school in Ireland and knowing little about the medieval oppression exercised there by the Catholic Church, he could not have realised that his life studies (including studies of naked models) would horrify the offcials who interviewed him. He was inevitably rejected and then set off during a hectic few months for a number of other interviews. Fettes College in Scotland saw him trying to get into the building through the wrong door and nearly causing havoc by ringing the founder's bell which was rung normally only once a year. That job failed to materialise as did one or two others for which he tried.

In *A Child Alone* he berates the welfare state for creating

Escaping to the greenwood is the central theme of *Brendon Chase*.

layabouts – pointing out that the grim necessities of earning a living faced him at this time with a stark choice: work or starve. He leaves out of this analysis the fact that only a tiny percentage of each generation during his early days could afford secondary education let alone a college course. And his allowance from his parents might have been small but it would have been the envy of most twenty-one-year-olds in the late 1920s with the Depression beginning to bite. But BB's political views, like so many of his views, were simply inherited and then held largely unmodified until his death. He was not a political animal at all and never questioned the ascendancy views he had imbibed from his parents. It should come as no surprise then that during the General Strike of 1926 he became a Special Constable and later joined the City of London Yeomanry. He would have thought it madness to even think about supporting the strikers against the establishment.

In 1928 the registrar at the Royal College of Art where BB was completing a year in the engraving schools sent for him and told him that he had heard that a job as assistant art master had come up at Rugby school. A few days later BB found himself being interviewed at one of Britain's best known public schools. He met the art master Talbot Kelly with whom he instantly established a rapport – 'he was as mad on birds as I was and we got on famously' – and on Kelly's advice the headmaster W.W.Vaughan, or the Bodger as he was known, offered BB the job.

It is very difficult to know if BB enjoyed teaching. He told me on different occasions that it was sometimes fun, or irksome or extremely tiring and dispiriting depending on his mood. Certainly he found it difficult at first because in that era the boys tended to think of art as something – to use BB's word – cissy. He also complained that schoolboys always smell like mice! But the fact that the boys saw art as something vaguely effeminate must have astonished BB who'd grown up with no interest in the traditional boys' enthusiasms for cars and football. What art meant was fixing the pleasures of nature on canvas or paper – how could any boy not be interested in that?

All his life BB drew and painted butterflies: this is from *Indian Summer*.

John Tremlett, a pupil at the school during BB's time remembered (in a letter to the BB Society journal) him smoking a pipe and dressed in a tweed jacket and brown corduroy trousers. He was apparently far less strict than Talbot Kelly the senior art master. Years later, in the 1960s, Tremlett wrote to BB asking if he remembered him: 'Yes,' came the reply, 'You were a scruffy little boy!'

If he occasionally disliked teaching it may have been at least partly because – ironically – being in the company of boys reminded him constantly that he was no longer one himself. Pushed out into the world of adulthood he could never forget his own words: 'Men never grow up and are always boys in their minds,' something he said to his friend Clive Sanger but that is somehow implicit in all his books.

Peter Craig, another of BB's pupils, remembered that the art room at Rugby was 'large and cavernous' and that BB gave the impression he did not enjoy his work. He left the class simply to get on with whatever work had been set.

The one recompense from teaching was that occasionally he taught a boy who had the same love of birds and of shooting and fishing and butterfly hunting. He went wildfowling every summer for a number of years with one particular favourite and his friendship with the boy lasted long after BB had given up teaching. Perhaps that relationship compensated however slightly for the loss of his own son Robin.

Much as BB loved his wife Cecily and daughter Angela there is no doubt that he always had a special affinity with boys. He may not have warmed to teaching but many years later he was still visiting local schools, but now as a celebrity local writer: he would arrive with bundles of signed copies of his books for the school library and was by all accounts instantly on the best of terms with the children.

# 7

# KICKING OVER
# THE TRACES

S OME TIME quite early on in his seventeen year (1928-1945)
teaching career BB began to write. He almost certainly
began by contributing articles to the weekly magazine
*Shooting Times* which he had taken on and off since he was a
boy. The magazine did not pay much for an occasional
countryside article but the fact that they paid at all no doubt
sowed a seed in BB's mind – that there was way to earn a living
and be free at the same time.

The fact that BB saw writing as an escape from earning a
living by teaching can be judged by his decision, in 1938, to
send not one but two manuscripts to a London literary agent,
David Higham. The books were *The Sportsman's Bedside Book*
and *Wild Lone, the Story of a Pytchley Fox*. When Higham, who
was to represent BB for the rest of his life, replied saying they
were happy to take him on and arrange for publication of 'the
book' BB was delighted but this was as nothing to the news
that arrived some time later from the publishers Eyre and
Spottiswood.

At this time he was still returning from his lodgings at
Rugby every weekend to stay with his parents at the rectory.
His father was now in failing health and he seems to have
been dismissive of his son's fledgling literary efforts. But BB
kept faith and each day of the holidays he waited:

The fox from *Wild Lone*: hunted but also admired and loved.

The weeks went by with no word from Eyre and Spottiswood, the publishers to which my agent had sent the mansucripts. Then one day Bob Dickens the postman brought me a letter with a London postmark – a letter I have carefully preserved for it was to me like a gleam of light at the end of a long tunnel. My secret ambition to be a writer as well as an artist seemed not so impossible after all.

With extraordinary luck the publishers had offered to publish not one but both his books – a wonderful spur to the fledgling career of any writer. He was also to illustrate the two books himself in conjunction with the artist G.D.Armour but these were early days and he tried etchings which did not work well, as he himself admitted. But already he was experimenting with the scraperboards that were to make his name: 'I found the medium ideal for book illustrations,' he tells us 'it was easy to reproduce and it was difficult to tell the finished effort from a woodcut print.'

More confident in himself at this time than he'd probably ever been, BB met and fell in love with a girl who shared his love of nature. She has never been identified but he was clearly smitten:

> Choosing the very worst possible moment to declare my feelings for her, resulted in us parting – both wounded and confused. She went abroad for a long stay. I thought I should hear from her but I never did.

He goes on to admit that he'd been demanding and jealous, unreasonable and 'plain stupid.'

The fact that the relationship ended seems to have been something of a spur to his writing career, however, and the idea for *Brendon Chase* – his own favourite of all his books – came to him. It is, as he said himself, an amalgam of Rugby School and his own adventures as a child:

I drew on my experiences as a boy when with my brother we used to camp in the wilds of Blueberry Bushes in the long summer holidays, taking with us a rifle with which we hunted for our meat and which we cooked over open fires.

The extent to which the world has changed since *Brendon Chase* was first published to acclaim in 1944 can be judged by the fact that the boys steal a rifle when they leave home and the book is full of descriptions of shooting animals and birds and in the case of the rabbits, eating their hearts and livers. *The Listener* magazine praised the book ('head and shoulders above most of this year's books') along with the *Times Literary Supplement*. Today there is no doubt that given the subject matter such a book would not find a publisher let alone be so widely reviewed.

But if *Brendon Chase* was BB's favourite book – largely because it epitomised his own magical childhood – *Little Grey Men* was the book that made his name. From the publication of the *Sportsman's Bedside Book* and *Wild Lone* in 1938, BB became immensely prolific and he was clearly working on, or at least thinking about *Brendon Chase* while working on *Little Grey Men*, and his later books often show evidence of re-cycling of material or stories from shooting or fishing books fictionalised for use in his children's stories.

BB was immensely hard working – Vera Freeman who worked as a maid for BB when he moved to Welford after his marriage in 1939 recalled that he always wrote in the dining room and when on one occasion she tapped nervously on the door to see if he was hungry – he'd been in there for hours without a break – he was amazed at how much time had passed.

Many memories of BB confuse times and places – Vera Freeman's memories make it sound as if BB had already stopped working at Rugby and was writing full time but in fact he was still at Rugby (if his own account is anything to go

Design for the paperback edition of *Little Grey Men*.

by) in 1942 and certainly stayed until 1945. In *A Child Alone* he recalls one of the greatest days of his life:

> Shortly after it (*Little Grey Men*) appeared in 1942 I was dumbfounded one day at Rugby to have a note from the headmaster complimenting me on winning the Carnegie Medal, which is awarded for the most outstanding children's book of the year.

*Little Grey Men* was also published in America and BB followed it with a sequel called *Down the Bright Stream. Little Grey Men* – for which later on Hollywood bought the film rights (though it never went into production) – is likely to be the book for which BB will be remembered longest. It's a simple story as BB himself acknowledged:

> I thought up a story of four little creatures, Sneezewort, Dodder, Cloudberry and Baldmoney who lived under an oak tree and how, years before Cloudberry the restless, more adventurous gnome had gone up the Folly Brook to find its source and never come back. His brothers decide to go in search of him. They build an ingenious boat with paddles, helped by their friends otter, kingfisher and vole. They undergo great peril from stoats and giant pike and worst of all from Giant Grum in the dark and evil shades of Crow Wood, through which ran the Folly Brook.

The creatures may now be gnomes rather than boys but the spirit of adventure, the immersion in nature and the motive of setting forth on a journey into the heart of the countryside is the central concern of this as of so many of BB's books.

By now he had realised that books about the countryside, fishing and shooting were not going to bring him fame and fortune. They were and are too narrow in their appeal and besides, as BB himself pointed out, 'writers about the country-side are always considered small beer.' Children's books were

The great adventure: from *Little Grey Men*.

another matter altogether for BB was writing them at the beginning of a revolution in publishing for children – a revolution that was eventually to produce the astonishing sales achieved by, among others, J.K.Rowling and Philip Pullman. Moving on to write more children's fiction was a shrewd move for a writer who wanted above all else to escape the humdrum of working nine to five. Like his brother Roger, BB was never really happy working for anyone other than himself.

In an interview in 1983 he confessed that having resigned from Rugby a few years after the success of *Little Grey Men* he found that funds quickly dried up and he had to work very hard to stay afloat – at one time he nearly had to move into a caravan and it was only his dedication and long hours at the typewriter, not to mention his wife Cecily's skill at making ends meet, that kept them going.

This may also explain why BB's writing career included at least one story (admittedly on fishing) written for the soft porn magazine *Men Only* as well as a few motoring features for a long defunct country magazine. He also sent illustrations to *The Countryman* magazine which had a huge circulation and a strict no hunting, shooting or fishing policy, but was widely read and hugely influential compared to other country magazines. It was also the only country magazine not obviously aimed at the very rich. BB found the comment made by his old art teacher that he could make a living as an illustrator was coming true – in between writing and illustrating his own books and articles he was to illustrate more than thirty (estimates vary) books by other writers.

By the early 1950s BB had long supported himself by his pen and he published his two wildfowling classics – *Tide's Ending* (1950) and *Dark Estuary* (1953 ). Both were well received in the shooting world but they were never likely to enjoy a big sale – wildfowling then as now was the sport of a tiny minority. The book was also one that BB knew might well upset many of those who bought his fiction and indeed his fishing books for he was still constantlyworking at several projects at once – *Confessions of a Carp Fisher* also came out in 1950 and through that year and every other year until his death some forty years later he wrote and drew regularly for *Shooting Times* and other magazines while working constantly on one or more books.

In an interview towards the end of his life he said he found his writing sometimes ran away with him and hours would fly by as he tapped out his stories. Lighter books of younger children's fiction poured from his pen – *The Forest of Boland Light Railway*, *Lepus the Brown Hare* and *Mr Bumstead* among others.

But despite the need for money and the fact that his children's books were always likely to be more lucrative than countryside books, he could not resist writing about some aspect or other of rural life or editing collections of countryside material. He rattled off the countryside books partly because they were relatively easy to do compared to the children's books and partly because he couldn't help himself: they provided work which made him happy because he believed that the next best thing to shooting and fishing and being in the countryside was reading, or in his case writing, about it. *Confessions of A Carp Fisher* is partly BB's own work and partly a collection of carp fishing stories by others. BB contributes a great deal but substantial chunks are by other writers and in later editions of the book the number of these sections by other writers increases. In the most recent edition Richard Walker's account of his record carp is included along with an account of the fifty-one pounder caught by Chris Yates who smashed Walker's carp record after more than forty years.

BB's first book, *The Sportsman's Bedside Book*, was followed over the years by other edited collections of favourite countryside and sporting prose: *The Countryman's Bedside Book*, *The Fisherman's Bedside Book*, *The Pegasus Book of the Countryside*, *The Naturalists's Bedside Book* and *Indian Summer*.

BB was a talented editor with a real eye for the quirky, the original, the exciting and well written short piece. He included what he himself loved which is what makes the collections so readable even today, but there is no doubt too that these were quick and easily compiled books that earned much needed cash.

By the early 1960s BB had turned to travel writing. This comes as a surprise to many who know only his fishing and countryside books and even more so to those who know only the children's books. The travel books – if that isn't too grand a term for them – include *The Autumn Road to the Isles, The White Road Westwards, The September Road to Caithness* and *Summer Road to Wales.*

Each recounts a journey BB made in summer with his old Land Rover and caravan. If they have not lasted as well as his other books the problem is not the quality of the writing; the difficulty is probably that travel writing has become as a genre a necessarily exotic affair – travel books about places we will never visit are the travel books that sell and the small scale domestic nature of BB's travel books have ensured that they have not been reprinted. That said they do contain some fine descriptive passages such as the following from *The September Road to Caithness* published in 1962:

> The headlights of cars went winking along the main Inverness road but on the narrow track below all was silent. I hoped to hear the roaring of stags from Glen Albyn behind me but all I could hear was the con-tinuous murmur of the waves coming up at me from the dusky loch below. A party of tits, even at this late hour, were busily hunting a clump of birch close by, but as the dusk closed in, welling like a tide, they vanished, no doubt to some well-loved hollow birch tree which was their nightly dormitory. Tits are very choosy over their bedrooms, and prefer a hole in a tree or a sheltered crevice in a rock to anywhere else.
>
> When darkness had come I lit a merry fire on the loch shore which soon blazed warm and bright. The wild perfume of the woodsmoke was like incense to

my nose. It brought back memories of former camps in this lovely land.

The sight and smell of a camp fire touches something deep down in most of us; it is part of man's earliest experience, for fire has brought comfort and succour to him down the ages.

I fetched my pipe from the van and sitting down on a flat stone I played upon it, and the low fret of waves and the sound of the autumn wind in the full-leaved alders made a fitting accompaniment.

Above me no stars shone, all was utter darkness . . . the night wind blew cold from off the water and I thought of wandering men who down the eternal procession of the years had sat beside this same loch shore beside a dying fire watching the black sticks turn to fiery gold, to rose pink and finally to grey ash, and smelled the wild rare tang of the camp fire's reek.

Slowly the fire died with minute rustlings and hissings. Louder seemed the echo of the clear wavelets beating on the smooth clean stones. The wind rustled among the dark leaves of the grove, a chill crept upon my back. Long after I had re-entered the lighted bay I saw, below there in the darkness, a faint radiance in the dying embers.

I have been unable to discover anything at all about a journey BB is said to have made before the war to Latvia and Lithuania – he went by cargo boat apparently – but clearly it did not inspire his pen. Nowhere in his journalism or other writing does he mention it. One other trip to Holland produced a magazine feature where he enthused over the avocets and spoonbills he saw, but his real travel interest lay much closer to home. His travel writing period was the early 1960s and this was no coincidence: he said in an interview that he sensed that the early 1960s would be the last period during which the countryside was generally speaking still recognisably the countryside he knew as a boy. The ragged hedgerows were already going – smashed into ugly straight even lines by mechnical flails (he lambasted these as bird killers on many occasions) or pulled out by farmers eager to make their fields bigger to increase their profits. Ponds were filled in too – they were just a nuisance in the brave new world of industrial farming – and odd corners of woodland came under the axe. Pesticides were also used indiscriminately by farmers and it was these pesticides – many, like DDT, later banned on the grounds that they were a serious health risk – that killed BB's wife, or so he always believed.

*The White Road Westwards* (1961) describes a journey BB made with his family towing their old caravan through Wiltshire, Hampshire, Dorset, Devon, Cornwall and Somerset. The journey lasted the length of one summer – roughly covering the period May to July 1960 – but it is full of wonderful descriptive passages, all with BB's special feeling for the magic of people and places.

> The sun sank lower, shining magically on pink foxglove spires. The sweet silence of the forest lapped us around, only the clear voices of the birds echoed and re-echoed, and from time to time the clarion call of a cock pheasant, an ugly unbirdlike sound, but one which is inseperable from large woodlands and great estates.
>
> We came upon a clearing where creamy skinned wattle hurdles, beautifully made, were piled one upon the other. A faint blue reek of woodsmoke hung in the air, for the forestry people were clearing some ground not far away and then, from out of the hazels a few yards in front of us, there stepped forth an exquisite sprite of the woods, a delicate being with slender legs, its coat the colour of a red squirrel, that ancient British woodland colour of fox and deer. The roebuck stopped in its tracks and turned its head, regarding us with eyes which were large and wondering and full of fear, two black liquid pools.

*The White Road* was followed in 1964 by *The Summer Road to Wales, The September Road to Caithness* (1962) and *The Autumn Road to the Isles* (1967). These are travel books only in a very limited sense for they are primarily books about nature: BB was fascinated by the birds, animals and trees of each region and he wanted to visit areas where his heroes had lived – in *The White Road Westwards*, for example, he visits Gilbert White's Selborne. Like so many of his books the travel volumes express BB's deep underlying conviction that nature has a deeper life than the life we see and hear – just as when he was a child in the big old rectory listening to the wind in the trees, he found the natural world of his travels not only beautiful but, occasionally even in England, terrifying. He sees ghosts and magical life in what most of us would see as an empty landscape, as in this extract from *The Autumn Road to the Isles*:

> But I was aware that from time to time above the ceaseless tumbling of the falls I clearly heard a curious 'clack' as of one large rock being struck against another, or of a stone being hit repeatedly with a hammer. The sounds were not regular, sometimes there was a minute's or so pause before I heard it again. I must confess I soon abandoned all idea of staying the night there alone, even with the company of a fire.

BB's travels in search of sport were much the same. The hardships of a long journey in winter to Scotland or East Anglia on a wildfowling trip never became too much to bear and in his eighties he visited Scotland regularly to lie out at night under the moon, even in the hardest January weather, waiting for the geese.

Perhaps his greatest wildfowling friend and companion was Douglas McDougall whose son Keith remembers, as a child, meeting BB:

BB was a friend and shooting companion of my father's for many years. Originally Douglas, my father, wrote to him as he was entranced by his magazine articles and asked if he could accompany him wild-fowling – this was in about 1945. Thereafter almost every year this intrepid duo met up and went to Perthshire to shoot, often with another of BB's friends Charles Oakey and Bill Humphries – also with myself and my brothers, Colin and Alan and also with the next generation, Douglas's grandsons!

So there was a lot of contact – good natured cama-raderie and leg-pulling. BB visited us in Norfolk. I remember him as one of my boyhood heroes – *Manka the Sky Gypsy* and *Wild Lone* set me off on a lifetime of BB worship.

Douglas, my father was a consumately good shot at geese using a double 8-bore. BB always used a magnum 12 bore – his attitude was a bit more laid back than Father's.

Both men were of their generation – gentleman sportsmen. Their delight was the wild surroundings, the moonlit expeditions and the simple comfort of local pubs who accommodated their irregular hours . . .

BB was a rather private man – a little serious, who attracted an element of leg-pulling by the McDougall siblings – but not in any way malicious. My dear mother could never get her tongue round his full name. She would say when introducing him: 'Now I would like you to meet Mr Watford-Pipkin'. It became a family joke. Poor BB. But we loved him. As a ten year old boy I rushed into the drawing room to show him my single barrelled .410. BB I clearly remember demonstrated every enthusiasm and encouragement to a small boy ecstatic with pride at his new weapon.

He was a very special human being – sometimes inclined to be patronising but then he had something

A rare departure from scraperboard illustration: this is from *Bill Badger and the Pirates*, (1960).

other sportsmen did not – a deep empathy with nature and a deep knowledge of natural history.

I think BB was deeply affected by the various tragedies in his family life – and like all writers he was driven by money problems. Some people thought him selfish and self centred. Maybe he was, a little, but I think it was triggered by his personal problems which he kept to himself. He did not unburden.

BB taught at Rugby for a little over seventeen years – roughly 1928 to 1945. From 1939, when he married, he lived in a house at Welford, a village close to the Northamptonshire boundary with Leicestershire and seems to have given it up and moved to Woodford Lodge only when he finally resigned from Rugby in the mid 1940s. But BB was notoriously unreliable about dates and locations: according to Vera Freeman who worked for BB and Cecily and their children he stayed at Welford until the mid 1950s and only then moved to Woodford Lodge which means that Robin must have died at Welford, yet in his own memoirs BB tells us that he went shooting in the woods at Woodford with Robin. The available evidence suggests that BB was at Welford until the mid 1950s and moved to Woodford when, financially speaking, his early successes with *Little Grey Men* and *Wild Lone* were not matched by later books like *Tide's Ending*.

'Through a kind friend' he tells us, he had been able 'to rent Woodford Lodge on a big estate not far from Lamport'. Here he returned to the habits of his childhood. The Richard Jefferies existence which, as a child he knew could not continue indefinitely had almost been recaptured. 'I had the run of the whole estate, a lake with an island which I stocked with fish and where we had picnics.'

In an interview in 1989 BB remembered that if the lodge had not been offered by a friend he had already decided that his finances were so bad that he would have to live in a caravan. But Woodford rescued him. Not only was it close to the scenes of his happiest childhood days but it was also a return

80

to the kind of freedoms he'd enjoyed as a child. He described himself at this time as free from the irksome instruction of boys who regarded art with little enthusiasm and felt 'free to do as I pleased.'

BB's wife Cecily came from a family of Northampton drapers and whether or not that business background had anything to do with it, she appears to have been very good indeed at making ends meet during what were often difficult financial periods. BB's two children Robin and Angela were born during the Welford years.

> I went fishing for trout and carp in the summer and shot pigeons in the woods in winter. It was wonderful shooting and I never came back empty handed. My son Robin had his own little pop gun and he always accompanied me to the pigeon wood loving every minute of it.

BB decorated the children's bedrooms at Welford with murals – Angela had scenes from nursery rhymes – Little Miss Muffett and Little Bo Peep while Robin had a large frieze running all the way around his room – it showed the poem 'There Was a Little Man Who Had a Little Gun'.

We know very little in detail about BB's relationship with Cecily – he always referred to her whether in print or conversation with the greatest affection and friends who knew the couple at various stages of their marriage confirm that theirs was indeed a very happy union. Apart from Cecily's financial skills she seems to be have enormously indulgent and was quite happy for BB to pursue his Richard Jefferies existence wandering the fields shooting and fishing. Despite their financial problems she never seems to have put pressure on him to get a job.

One rare and delightful moment in *The Autumn Road to the Isles* does give us a glimpse of the couple, but this was before her premature death in 1974. After 1974 he became extremely reticent, but through his earlier published recollections of a happy summer we get a snapshot of the couple on holiday with their pet peke:

> For the last few nights, Ping, having been put on the spare bunk and covered with her little blanket (she slept like an infant on her side with her head pillowed on her cushion), took to getting into our bed at 3 am, a performance which invariably woke us up. It was a form of blackmail, for we decided that henceforth she had better sleep with us for the duration of the trip. She is an extremely jealous little person and if I so much as kissed my wife good morning as she lay beside me in bed, Ping was between us in a moment, placing her two front paws and then her round soft head between our faces. Any affectionate demonstration brought immediate reactions. Even when she was at the far end of the van she would jump down and place herself between us as if to say, `No more of this, I'm the only one to have any affection!' One great mystery was never solved by her — where we went when we withdrew to the lavatory compartment. She would sit with her round grapefruit head tilting first one side, and then the other, an anxious expression on her face.

Happy in his marriage and freed from the chores of a nine to five existence BB experienced a return to the idyll of childhood but the bliss of these post Rugby days was shattered when Robin became ill with Bright's Disease, a rare affliction of the kidneys. Though BB said in *A Child Alone* that he would never write about the death of his son he did write about it in a letter to his friend Ronald Clough. The passage about Robin is unbearably poignant even today: 'My little boy is gravely ill, pray for him, Robin seven years.' A little while later Clough received another letter: 'My dearest son died in my arms in the early hours of November 6. I do not think life will ever be the same again for me.'

Woodford Lodge, like the house at Welford, was no mere cottage. Three stories and built in a pale grey stone it provided BB with a long studio on the second floor where he could work undisturbed. In the garden he set up aviaries where he kept bullfinches – he had kept them as pets since he was a child and in his late eighties still had one in a cage in his sitting room at the Round House. To the end of his life talk of 'bullies' and the various individual birds he'd known over the decades always produced a look of real pleasure on a face that increasingly bore the signs of ineradicable sadness. It was also at Woodford that he first set up the netted cages in which, for decades, he was to hatch the eggs of the purple emperor butterfly in an almost single handed effort to save this large beautiful insect from extinction.

When BB wrote about the purple emperor in the now defunct magazine *Gamekeeper and Countryside* he was worried that it would soon be gone for good from its few Northamptonshire strongholds. He would no doubt be delighted that his efforts to save this rare insect mean that it is still there: a group of BB enthusiasts on a butterfly spotting trip in BB's old haunts in Salcey Wood in 2003 spotted a number of emperors flitting through the high tops of the trees.

In the very different world that BB had known as a child butterflies were there to be hunted – he and Roger spent long days catching and mounting specimens, but as the years wore on pesticides took their deadly toll and like so many men of his generation he became something of a poacher turned gamekeepeer when it came to butterflies.

Like fishing and shooting, butterflies were something for which he never lost his enthusiasm. As a boy he'd read about

BB never tired of trying to capture the pleasure and excitement of water. This is from *Little Grey Men*.

the large blue and set off on his bicycle hoping to see (and no doubt catch) one despite the fact that it had not been seen in Northamptonshire by then for more than fifty years, but through his fishing books, children's fiction and travel books the love of butterflies is clear – the comma reminds him of an 'unripe blackberry'; and he writes of the silver washed fritillary's 'rich tawny gold wings'. But it wasn't only rarities that gave him pleasure and he was as delighted to see huge numbers of the common cabbage white dancing above the fields. He travelled up to Wicken Fen in Cambridgeshire on several occasions to see the large copper and writes rapturously about the brimstone butterflies that he looked forward to seeing each year almost as much as he loved to see the first swallow.

Away from shooting and fishing all of nature seems to have interested BB from the light falling at evening to the curiously twisted ivy on a dead oak tree; from the gleaming ranunculus waving over gravel beds in some tiny Midland stream to the wild bleak heather moorlands of Scotland.

The 1950s and 60s seem to have been a lean time for BB – he wrote regularly for several magazines to keep his head financially above water and though his book sales were steady, nothing seems to have matched the early successes of *Little Grey Men* and *Brendon Chase*.

In the 1970s, however, things took a turn for the better when Southern TV made a series based on *Brendon Chase* – Southern TV was eventually bought by an Australian media company who appear to have kept the master tapes of the series but it has yet to be issued as a DVD or video.

*Lord of the Forest* produced some of BB's finest artwork.

The history of BB's relationship with television and film is interesting – he loved turning up unannounced when the television series of *Brendon Chase* was being filmed and was particularly impressed by the care with which each part was cast. He also loved the re-creation of Smokoe Joe's den.

By the early 1980s Hollywood was even showing some interest, but not in *Brendon Chase*. As BB wrote to a friend: 'My *Little Grey Men* is due to appear as a full length film in the USA with Julie Andrews. I have just signed up the second option for a hefty fee, the Yanks do not seem to mind how much money they spend.' In the event the film was never made but the Hollywood film company that bought the option on the book still retains that option which means that we might yet see Sneezewort and Cloudberry on the big screen.

# 8

# SHOOTING DAYS

B B himself admitted that many people who knew and loved his countryside and children's books were sometimes shocked when they discovered that the man who wrote so sensitively about nature and animals was also a keen shooting man.

The changing tide of opinion about shooting in particular – fishing seems to have escaped similar censure – did affect BB, although he defended shooting until the end. If he'd ever felt that the modern world was placing various species – or the natural environment generally – under intolerable pressure there is no doubt he would have given shooting up completely. We have only to compare the situation in his lifetime with butterflies. Once he realised that butterflies were seriously threatened he gave up hunting them and, as we have seen, did his utmost to improve their chances of survival. He was never a great one for big formal pheasant shooting days but just as the boys in *Brendon Chase* loved the idea that with rod and gun they could bag something for the pot and survive like outlaws, BB never lost the sense that he could be, at least to some extent, self sufficient.

He told me during one journey across Northamptonshire to visit many of his old haunts that there was a particular satisfaction to be had from shooting or catching something and taking it home to eat. He liked the idea of wild food – food untouched by those hated farm sprays and chemicals and the praise that must have greeted him when as a child he returned

Fishing with a float never failed to recapture the joy of boyhood. An illustration from *Fisherman's Folly*.

with a basket of perch or a rabbit was probably echoed by Cecily's delight at his return from the fields in middle age with similar spoils.

But as Keith McDougall points out BB was always rather laid back when it came to shooting – what I think was meant by this was that BB did not make any particular effort to become a great shot; he didn't care to bag large numbers of anything – birds or fish or rabbits. As he grew older this tendency grew and he came to love the atmosphere of the hunt, as it were, more than the hunt itself – when he fished he used only a few flies and never bothered to become a 'scientific' angler like his great friend Richard Walker.

BB was a founder member of the Carp Catchers' Club but would have had little interest in the rows of hi-tech carbon rods and electronic buzzer alarms that now line the banks of carp lakes up and down the country. In fact he never even showed much interest in even vaguely modern techniques – very few serious carp fishers, even in the 1950s and 60s, would have used an old fashioned float, for example, but for BB fishing without a float took most of the fun out of it. The boyhood sight of a thin red-tipped quill disappearing into the green depths as a fish took hold of the bait somewhere down below was a central part of the pleasure of fishing – bite alarms and legered baits that gave the angler nothing to look at were a poor substitute and it didn't matter how often it was proved that freelined and legered baits were more effective.

But it is testimony to BB's tolerant nature that he could go his own way while allowing others to do just the same. Richard Walker became one of the greatest exponents of scientific fishing; BB liked to fish as he did when he was a boy, but the two remained friends until Walker's death in 1985. And whenever he fished, one of the greatest pleasures for BB was camping out by the water and cooking a few of the fish they caught – he had a particular relish, recalls one friend, for eels!

BB's attitude to shooting was very similar – he didn't take shooting lessons; he didn't buy the latest gear or try out fancy new approaches. He shot as he'd shot as a boy wandering the fields with his dog at heel and hoping to take something home for the pot.

Shooting certainly inspired some of his most heartfelt writing, as in this extract from *The Sportsman's Bedside Book* (1937):

I had an interesting experience last night. With my old fowler as guide, we went out under the moon after the barnacle geese. We walked about three miles in our heavy gear and arrived at the merse at 11.35 p.m. For a while we stood listening for the geese, and eventually heard them about half a mile off.

We walked towards the sound for some time until it became fairly loud. Then we took to hands and knees and finally stomach-crawled. The frost thickly rimed the herbage on the merse and in a short time our hands were frozen stiff. Nearer came the sound until I could hear the cooing undertones of the geese.

The stalk had taken quite an hour and we were both very cold. I looked at my watch and found it was nearly 3.30. The moon shone down and glistened on the marsh herbage and along our guns. The flock — the main barnacle army — appeared to be just over the merse edge and it seemed to me that they were feeding away from us. I counselled J to crawl back and head them off.

Hardly had he begun his journey, however, when there was a great roar. The whole pack was up, baying to the moon. J growled, `Let goo, Sirr; let goo!' and four shots rang out. But no bird fell, and we stood listening to the geese go out across the bay until the sounds died away.

The moon was sliding down towards the mountains, and the sky was dusted with frosty stars. J stood looking and listening, his shadow black in the moon-light behind him. 'They'll be awa to the river mooth nae doot, and will no feed the night again'.

Woodcock in winter: from *Ramblings of a Sportsman Naturalist*.

There's no doubt that for BB the pleasure of shooting had as much to do with being in wild places as it had to do with actually firing a gun and he was still planning an expedition to Scotland when he was already very ill with the kidney complaint that was to kill him, but I think fishing was his greatest love because it combined earliest happiness with a love of bringing something home for the pot, but both combined with a love of the mystery of water.

He often said that water had a curiously profound effect on him and he could hardly pass a bridge or culvert without stopping to gaze down for long minutes into the water below. Lochs, small streams, lakes and wide rivers were all equally compelling. It was the sense of the unknown beneath the surface that was endlessly fascinating – even the smallest stream might harbour monstrous fish.

One of the most famous passages from *Confessions of a Carp Fisher* has all the atmosphere of BB's best writing about water and fishing:

When I look back upon all the carp waters I have fished in my life, the old copper mine takes premier place in my affections, or rather, I should say, it exerts upon me the greatest influence, and imprints its picture most fixedly on my mind. It is a sinister place yet powerfully fascinating. You turn off the main road which hums with busy traffic, by a little thatched house as cosy as a wren's nest, its whitewashed walls and latticed casements reminding one of a fairy house in a fairy wood – one almost expects a bear to be looking out of the window or a little withered witch in a steeple hat and scarlet cloak.

The winding lane (why are all the good carp waters I have known reached by little lanes?) goes up the hill, scarcely wide enough to allow the passage of a car, certainly not sufficient for two to pass each other. The strange thing is that for some years I used to visit friends of mine who lived within a few miles of

Beechmere Pool (for such is its name) and I had never known of its existence!

I followed the lane to the top where there is an old tumbledown barn and, passing through the barn yard, I still could see no sign of any pool and wondered if I had come to the wrong place. Before me the ground fell away almost sheer, clothed thickly with oaks and it was not until I descended the bank by a crooked, slippery path in the clay that I glimpsed the glimmer of the pool shining dimly through the trees at my very feet. Soon I saw its full expanse and beauty. It was a great square of dark water of about four or five acres, surrounded on all sides by high banks which were clothed on the right by oaks and on the left by magnificent beeches which came right down the steep sloping bank to the water's edge, their knotted and snaky grey roots protruding from the soil.

The August evening was overcast, not a breath of wind rustled in the trees and a deathly stillness brooded there and yet, as I listened, I realised that there was in the air a strange and fevered humming caused by the myriads of insects in the trees about. A path ran all round the pool, a slippery and dangerous path which wound its way over roots and round trees. In places it was twenty feet above the surface of the water, in others it came about level with it, evidently a fisherman's path.

The sloping walls of this gigantic well dived straight down into the black water – one slip upon the path in several places would have precipitated the unwary angler into unknown and terrifying depths, indeed it is said that in the middle this strange pool is two hundred feet deep.

Its history which I learned later is as follows. About a century ago it was a flourishing and busy place – a copper mine, resounding to the rumble of barrow and rattle of picks and shovels. One night the workmen went home as usual, tired no doubt with their day's work. On their return next morning an amazing transformation had taken place.

During the hours of darkness a subterranean stream had burst forth from the bowels of the mine and was rapidly flooding the whole working. Barrows and other implements were already submerged and the water won rapidly, gallery by gallery until, in a very short space of time, it was full to its very brim, the stream finding an exit half way down the western side. It was beyond human ingenuity to pump the water out – indeed the whole thing had happened so swiftly and suddenly, there had been no time to combat this onrush of water and so it has remained to this day.

Some years after, a local man put in a number of carp – nobody quite knows exactly when the fish were introduced – and they have been left pretty well to their own devices.

# 9

# LAST DAYS

B Y 1968 WHEN BB, Cecily and Angela had moved into the Round House at Sudborough still less than twenty miles from BB's childhood home, he was an established figure with a small but loyal following. His books appealed – to use his agent's own words – to people of a certain age. Already he'd become something of an anachronism – as the growth in children's fiction became an explosion, books like *Little Grey Men* and *Brendon Chase* came to seem rather old-fashioned. BB's children suddenly seemed too obviously public school and dated. But that said his *Bill Badger* series and *Lepus the Wild Hare* were translated into Japanese (various of his books were translated into seven different languages in all) and older people continued to buy his books for their children and grandchildren.

Carp fishermen and others still wanted his fishing books, which were reissued although usually by smaller publishers and in far smaller numbers. The appeal was that of the classic – *Confessions of a Carp Fisher* had become legendary simply because it was the first book to establish the character of the carp fisherman and in many ways carp fishermen began to live up to the image created by BB. They stayed for weeks at a time by the water's edge, stopped shaving and washing and culti-vated a haunted obsessive stare.

Not all BB's ideas about the nature of the fisherman were probably accurate – there is a wonderful sentence in *Confessions* where he insists that hairdressers make particularly good fishermen. What evidence he had for this is not known!

Journeying forth: an illustration from the Carnegie Medal winning
*Little Grey Men*.

But by now he was in his late sixties and though he still shot and fished he had moved on. He nursed a goose he'd shot back to health and kept it as a pet; he was continually rearing numbers of bullfinches along with purple emperor butterflies and he had two ponds dug at the back of the Round House so that rather than kill an occasional big carp he could release it but keep it close by.

Big Pond can't have been more than twenty-five feet long and Little Pond was a typical small garden pond. But BB put a big common carp in the larger of the two and fed it each day with bread paste balls. He would always take visitors – and there were quite a few, if intermittent visitors now – to see the carp and to sit for a while at the side of the pond.

He was proud, too, of his netted sallow trees where the purple emperor eggs he collected with such care could be safely hatched and then released back into Salcey forest. Though his eyesight was already poor at least in one eye he continued to paint and produce scraperboards which he offered to visitors at £10 each – one wonders how many visitors turned down the offer only to regret it later for even the smallest scraperboards now fetch hundreds of pounds.

One of the more endearing features of BB's old age was his honest awareness of his own limitations – he kept painting and drawing for the fun of it, but admitted that with his failing sight his work was no longer what it had once been. But he was a tough character who wouldn't give up and, like his father all those years ago, he liked to be busy with plans and new ideas – not for cars and mechanical devices but for outings in search of fish or butterflies or geese.

Like many countrymen of his generation he also loved to be surrounded by animals – in fact he found it impossible to be without a dog and was rarely without a caged bird or two.

He'd once accidentally shot a favourite dog and was brave enough to write about it, but he was not sentimental and if a dog was hopeless or badly behaved when he took it out shooting he would get rid of it.

Big Pond

BB's own carp pond at the Round House, illustrated in *Indian Summer*.

After one of his first dogs, Sport, died in 1937 he wrote in his regular magazine column:

> I am in that miserable state, the dogless state, that must be well known to many sportsmen. I am looking for a successor to my old friend Sport, and up to the present moment I have been unsuccessful. One labrador I have had on trial has proved a failure. She looked a nice bitch and would retrieve the dummy from land or water, but as soon as she saw my gun she fled in abject fear, tail between legs. My old spaniel was a dog of such character that I think I may never get another that will equal him. He had faults; mainly that he was noisy, but this was perhaps his only drawback.
>
> Has it ever occurred to you that one can judge people by their dogs, that dogs are very good guides to character? The maiden lady's dog (usually a little bad-mannered), the fussy man's dog, the non sporting man's dog, the mean man's dog, the arty man's dog; they are all to be found. Dull people have dull dogs. The reason is obvious. A dog absorbs something of his master's characteristics. They are very receptive animals.

He often wrote about these problems in the hope that a kind reader would help him out and in fact this often happened – when his right eye packed up completely a reader provided him with an extraordinary looking shotgun with a cross over stock and at least one dog turned up as a result of a reader response to BB's latest predicament.

For BB of course a dog wasn't just a shooting companion; like his carp Big Boy, his bullfinches and his tame goose it was a much loved pet and pets, like the countryside, were an integral part of his childhood and adulthood.

His description of his pet linnet in *The Countryman's Bedside Book* (1941) is one of the most delightful things he ever wrote and it is enormously revealing about the man who was at heart still a boy:

I fed the linnet on brown bread soaked in scalded milk (white bread will soon kill any bird of the finch family), crushed rape seed and boiled hemp. The hemp was boiled in a rag until the seed, which is rather like a tiny white bulb, split out of the round shell. Small particles of hard-boiled egg — the yolk, not the white — is also good, but too much causes constipation. Young birds are like trees or plants which have been dug up and removed to a new place. Some will die however much you work, others, after a few days (whilst their stomachs are adjusting themselves to the unaccustomed food) will thrive. My little linnet managed to survive and one day she cracked her first seed and I knew she would be safe.

Very soon she became so tame that when I opened the cage door she immediately flew out and perched on my shoulder and very soon she developed a character. One or two games she loved to play. Whilst I was writing she would sidle across the table and, waiting her chance, seize hold of the nib of the pen. If this failed she would take hold of the corner of the paper and carry it to the edge of the table and drop it over, standing on the very edge with side-cocked head watching its wavering flight to the floor below. This was quite a feat for so diminutive a bird. Another game was to climb up the collar of my coat and nibble the short hairs in the nape of my neck. Perching on the rim of the collar she would seize a hair in her bill and tug for all she was worth, going back on her heels and putting all her strength in the effort. Sometimes too she would sit directly under my ear and hop up my face; her little feet were always very warm. Then she would preen my eyebrows, putting each hair in place. The curious thing about this trick was that she never attempted to pull out an eyebrow hair.

Like all wild birds she loved her bath, which she took in a saucer set on the floor. She soon got to know my step and had a special call note as soon as she heard me enter the house. She could distinguish between my step and another's, even from a distance, and she would fly to no one else.

If I walked gently about the room she rode on my shoulder and seemed to enjoy it, though if I quickened my pace or made any swift motion, she flew off. Birds hate any sudden movement and will never become attached to anyone who does not walk or move with a smooth and calculated tread.

She lived for eight years and then one day, when I opened the door of the cage, I saw she was sick. Her feathers were puffed and crest raised. A bird will only raise its head feathers when it is angry, pleased, or ill. The tiny eyes, usually so full and bright and smiling, were like little agates and half their usual size. She flopped out of the cage and rolled into my hand and I felt the little body was chill. There she died and my heart ached with heavy sorrow, a sorrow which remained for weeks.

BB was enormously caring about all kinds of animals even though in some cases he also shot and ate them. He had a particular fondness for hedgehogs and the following comes from *The Autumn Road to the Isles*.

'What a darling!' exclaimed Cecily, 'but what's he doing in the road?' I brought Winston, the Land Rover, to a halt, got out, and lifted the hedgehog up.

'I don't think he's too well,' I said. The little animal did not seem to be unduly alarmed and made little effort to curl up, which was a bad sign.

When I put him on my lap, and gently pressed his forehead prickles, he unrolled completely. I have a way with hedgehogs and they understand me, but this one seemed unusually insensitive. I had noticed over the last few days numberless carcasses of young hedgehogs flattened on the mountain roads, especially in those places where bracken fringed the sides and woods came close. Perhaps they were looking for their winter hibernation quarters, for in late autumn they become restless. I was aware, too, that we had had some hard frosts of late, and now the frost had gone and the sun shone warmly the hedgehogs had, no doubt, re-emerged, like wasps and flies do on a warm day in late autumn. Usually when this takes place it bodes ill for them, for this sun of late October is treacherous, temperatures can drop in a matter of minutes, and hard frosts may strike suddenly at night.

'What shall we do with him?' asked Cecily, stroking his head prickles.

'Take him along with us,' I said. 'We'll fix up a box for him when we get to Bonar Bridge. I'll get him some bracken, and he'll be as snug as a flea under a dog's ear.' So I tucked him inside my coat where he crawled against my left side and lay still, in the warm and the dark.

Ping's round head appeared over my shoulder. Little silver bubbles decorated the ends of her whiskers. She could smell the newcomer and was determined to investigate. Hedgehogs must possess a most appetising smell for dogs, for it seems to drive them frantic. Possibly they smell of tender pork; no doubt they taste very like it too.

Many times I have wanted to taste hedgehog and have even caught one, intending to devour it. My heart has always quailed at the thought of administering the coup de grace. In any case, I don't know how one would kill a hedgehog humanely.

We stopped at an hotel for a meal and brought Bonny in from the Land Rover and put him on the table where he soon ran about and ate some bread and milk with much relish. He made as much noise over this as a bearded old man drinking soup. Ping, who was asleep, suspected that I was kissing Cecily. She rose up in wrath to come and separate us and had to be restrained.

Those who knew BB in the last years of his life were probably not aware of his great sense of fun – as a child he'd loved the rough and tumble of games and pranks (despite his supposed delicate constitution) and something of this lasted if not into his extreme old age then at least into his sixties and seventies – on his annual jaunts in the Land Rover and caravan he liked the fact that his pet animals sometimes seemed to bully him; he enjoyed it when things went wrong or he and Cecily got in a muddle or lost their way because it all made good copy for his magazine articles and books and though he never presented himself in his work as a complete buffoon he liked to run himself down and make jokes at his own expense.

This appears frequently in his autobiography – at every turn we are told that his teachers at The Royal College of Art thought of him as a 'nit wit'; and when he went for his first job interviews he loves to tell the tale of his mistakes – trying the wrong door, misunderstanding instructions and so on. BB's relaxed attitude to travel matches his relaxed attitude to shooting and fishing. He wanted to succeed, certainly, but only on his own terms. He loved travel, fishing and shooting but only because they were as much a part of his inner life as his relationship with Cecily and his pets.

The early 1970s were a busy time – if his own books were selling fewer copies at least he'd written so many that the aggregate of sales still provided a living. He was also illustrating more work by others and continued to sell paintings locally. Then, in 1974, came a disaster to match that of the death of Robin. Cecily, his wife of more than thirty years, had been working in the garden when she came back into the house feeling unwell. She said that the farmer had been spraying the fields on the other side of the garden hedge and that the spray had blown into the garden and completely covered her. She began almost immediately to feel unwell. Within a few weeks she was dead.

Outside the Round House by Big Pond.

BB had always hated modern industrial farming which destroyed butterflies, insects and birds but the death of his wife confirmed his loathing of yet another aspect of the modern world. Cecily had not only been the emotional main-stay of his life and his companion in their annual summer travels but she had managed their precarious finances with almost miraculous skill. BB was so distressed that for a while even Northamptonshire and its countryside could not console him. He wrote to Colonel Lancaster, a local landowner, who had written to express his sadness on hearing of Cecily's death:

How good of you to write. I can now only hope to lose myself in my creative work and forget the tragedy – and later to leave this county and go somewhere – probably Shropshire – where there is less agriculture and artifical aids – somewhere I can still find the wildlife I knew as a boy.

Of course, as we know, the pull of his own childhood lost now among the changed fields was too strong and that move to Shropshire never took place. This disaster was followed in 1975 by the good news that *Little Grey Men* was to be broadcast on radio that year and Southern TV's version of *Brendon Chase*, shown in 1981, was eventually sold to fourteen countries. By now there had also been American editions of *Little Grey Men*, *Brendon Chase*, *Wild Lone* and other books – *Confessions of a Carp Fisher* was never published in America which is hardly surprising given that in the USA the carp is considered a terrific pest.

The 1980s saw the gradual emergence of the idea that BB was

Roger Watkins-Pitchford, BB's twin, became a successful broadcaster in Canada.

the grand old man of country writing. Parties of shy Japanese tourists occasionally besieged him and at other times small groups of carp fishers would turn up to meet the legendary author of *Confessions*.

Chris Yates, who broke the long standing carp record held from 1952 by BB's friend Richard Walker, turned up to present BB with a silver salver. He had become the father of modern fishing. Journalists wrote about him more often now, and friends helped when he found it increasingly difficult to drive.

In 1986 Roger, his twin, returned from Canada after more than half a century and moved to the Round House. The brothers got on well as BB always said they had as children – the special bond between twins meant that it didn't really matter how long they were apart since they could always easily pick up the threads when they were together again. Roger spent his days tending a vegetable patch at the back of the garden while BB looked after his carp pond and his purple emperor cages. Roger seems to have returned from Canada with very little to show for his years there – if BB had not taken him in it is difficult to know what he would have done. The old competitive spirit between the two boys clearly still existed and a number of interviewers noted Roger's tendency to chip in and bring the conversation round to himself. BB once confided to me after a long almost obsessive interlude during which Roger talked about his time in Canada that it was because Roger felt that he had failed somehow. BB thought this was a pity and that Roger was entirely underestimating his achievements – in fact Roger had been a well known broadcaster in Canada.

Then one morning in 1988 BB took Roger a cup of tea as he did every morning and he found his brother had died in the night. There seemed something inevitable about this death and though BB was deeply upset by the loss it had come at the end of a life marked by loss. He was innured now to suffering. There was something inevitable now about death and BB probably knew that he did not have long to live himself. By the late 1980s he needed regular dialysis treatment as his kidneys were

Salmon from *Confessions of a Carp Fisher*, one of the greatest of all books on fishing.

only partially functioning – ironic given that kidney disease had killed Robin all those years ago.

But BB was never alone in these last days. Fans of his books wrote regularly to him and he had a wide circle of aquaintances with whom he conducted an intermittent correspondence. He replied to every letter without fail, always polite, always interested; he still saw old friends like Douglas McDougall but less often now. Visitors frequently turned up with great piles of his books and asked if he would sign them – BB, unfailingly polite, would always oblige. One of his most endearing traits was that he never for a minute took his fame, such as it was, for granted. He relished to the end the pleasure that his books gave and he never grew to despise his fans – something that is common among more famous writers.

Visitors were always given tea and a tour of the house and garden – the tour would have been just what BB would have offered visitors sixty years earlier at the Rectory. Sheila Bradshawe, looking back in 2000, remembered the Watkins-Pitchfords in 1916. She was nine at the time and recalled a musical afternoon at Lamport:

> The Reverend Watkins-Pitchford, called Bru by his wife, had composed and compered musical pro-grammes in the early days of the wireless. That afternoon he played the piano and my mother and Denys's twin brother Roger sang. I believe Mrs Watkins-Pitchford played violin. Denys not being musical and probably prompted by his mother, took me to see the garden. I remember the lily pond and finding a bird's nest.

At the end of his life a tour of the garden was still a favourite outing and the natural gesture of a good host.

BB was much photographed in his last decade but I have been unable to find a single photograph in which he is smiling. I took more than one hundred photographs of him between

1985 and 1989 and in not one is there the glimmer of a smile. In fact the sorrows of his life are etched on his face in all these late pictures, but in conversation he still smiled (or twinkled might be a better description) and his enthusiasm for the countryside was undimmed. He also liked to play chess now and then although as his friend and driver Clive Sanger remembered he was a terrible cheat although he would instantly admit what he'd been up to if he was caught. Throughout his adult life he had smoked a pipe and once wrote a magazine feature extolling the virtues of tobacco:

> My pipe is part and parcel of my enjoyment of the countryside. It is thickset briar root, coloured like a ripe chestnut conker, so it always gives a cool smoke. It is just right in the hand and easy to hold. It has a chubby aspect and is well crusted. The tobacco which is cooked in it gives a superb and mild smoke.

BB's skill with the pen was clearly also undiminished – that lovely conceit of tobacco being cooked in the briar is so much more evocative than merely saying that the tobacco was smoked in the pipe.

Some of his correspondents wanted practical advice: Gordon Wright remembered telephoning BB after finding an abandoned nest of young bullfinches. BB replied by return:

> After your phone call I thought I would rush this letter off to you and with luck your bullfinch brood will still be alive. The hedgerow you describe, sadly, is now an ever growing feature of our countryside. It's a quick means of topping but the mechanical blade just tears through the hedge and any birds and wildlife in the way are doomed. It is best to keep the brood in a box with a top and ideally, if you managed to salvage it, still in the hair nest, most important to keep them warm at night. I use a chicken lamp but warm flannel will do to lie over the brood.

There follows an elaborate recipe for crushed boiled rapeseed and instructions to feed the brood every hour every day from 6 a.m. to sunset. BB's assumption throughout is that no one could possibly imagine not going through the long hard slog to ensure the birds' survival.

BB himself allowed his numerous pet bullfinches to fly around the house freely. He almost always had bird droppings on the shoulder of his coats but would have thought it the height of absurdity to be upset or the least disturbed by this. It was nothing when set against the company of a bullfinch. He once took a favourite to the vet that had broken its leg and paid for an expensive operation to amputate the damaged leg which would not mend. He wrote:

> Rearing a brood you come to find that birds are cerrtainly not what you first thought them to be; they are a little like wild woodland children, yet they do not fret when put into captivity. I am devoted to my little bullycock Piper and he is to me. I hear he is moping since I have been away.

And the hold that the purple emperor had on BB was quite remarkable. As a boy he'd stared endlessly at pictures of the beautiful insect in Frohawk's *British Butterflies* and he was inspired to begin searching for purple emperors when he discovered that one of its chief haunts was Northamptonshire. What began as a fascination was to become almost an obsession. BB trained his daughter Angela to look for the tiny eggs and she became a superb hunter – BB had stopped hunting for specimens to collect and wanted specimens to save. It wasn't until 1946 that he first discovered a rich and reliable purple emperor habitat and it was in Oxfordshire. Salcey Forest in Northamptonshire later became a favourite haunt of BB's for it was an excellent place to see purple emperors – perfect that is until deadly chemical sprays used to eliminate oak moths in the 1950s, made the poor purple emperors extinct. In the 1950s it seems only a few brave souls like BB stood out against this kind of wanton destruction. But by the 1970s when the tide had turned against the destruction of the countryside BB had long been doing his bit. He was releasing dozens of hatched insects into the emperor's old haunts at Salcey Forest and elsewhere.

By the late 1990s, almost a decade after BB's death, purple emperors – extinct in most of Northamptonshire until BB started his work – were seen again regularly in the county. They were even seen dancing in the tree tops one summer near the Round House. How delighted BB would have been. And still as he reached the last year of his life the fishermen came – one wanted to photograph BB with the rod and reel Richard Walker had made for him and BB was, as always, happy to pose for pictures but looking out now at the lens like a character lost in an unfamiliar world.

Writers and artists are often judged harshly when early promise fails to turn into something exceptional. Augustus John, the artistic genius of the 1890s and BB's own favourite artist, is a good example. The huge promise of his early years did not develop into mature genius and his vast output in the 1920s and beyond revealed only an empty and largely commercial vision. BB, unlike his hero, was never lionised or told that he was an artistic genius; but like the greatest artists and writers he stuck to his early vision and developed it through a long life. He certainly worked with money in mind but he had no interest in writing about the countryside to a brief – he would have thought it absurd to be asked, for example, to write a feature in praise of modern farming; or to write a magazine article arguing in favour of adding huge numbers of modern houses to old villages. BB's vision and interests may have been limited but they were uniquely his.

His children's books may have been unfashionable in the 1970s and 1980s but fashion in writing as in art and music is a cyclical thing. Many artists find that their reputation slumps, sometimes for decades, after their deaths. Time then sends up new shoots of interest and the virtues of a long forgotten artist and writer are re-discovered by a new generation.

BB was quietly confident that his books would never be completely forgotten and that his art would come to be judged for its unique vision. In many ways his quiet confidence has been justified in recent years. BB would have loved the fact that one of the greatest modern children's authors, Phillip Pullman, described a new edition of *Brendon Chase*, released in 2000, as 'brimming with delight'.

I last met BB in July 1989. He had little more than a year to live. When I arrived at the Round House he was in his usual friendly crumpled state but unusually animated. He'd written a curious letter telling me that 'there may be an important item concerning me and my career which will have to go in your book'.

I was mystified but at the Round House nothing had changed. His bullfinch still happily flitted about the sitting room and what was to be his last and now rather arthritic dog lay on the floor nearby wheezing heavily. The long case clock ticked and the pictures – including his own copy of Velasquez's Philip – still hung awkwardly on the gently curving walls. By now the house was seriously dilapidated ('Like me it isn't as young as it was,' he said with a sad smile)

BB and daughter Angela.

and there were large cracks in the ceiling. After BB's death the new owner told me that it was a miracle the house hadn't collapsed during BB's time as nothing seemed to be holding up the ceilings and walls. Extensive repairs were necessary but the new owner is an admirer of BB's work and has kept as much as possible of the original fabric of the house.

We had the usual tour of the garden and Angela joined us on the bench overlooking Big Pond. For some reason Big Boy was not in a playful mood and would not come to the surface to be fed. In the studio I saw an unfinished oil on which BB had been working – considering he was by now almost blind it had a curiously assured feel to it. The netted sallows were still there too in the garden and BB was able to point out the tiny eggs; we had tea and Angela extolled as usual the cold preventing virtues of raw onions.

BB had been awarded an Honorary MA by Leicester University in 1986 – something of which he was enormously proud, but as we walked around the garden I could tell that he wanted to tell me something. We finished our tour and sat together in the siting room. No longer able to contain his excitement he said he had been contacted by Buckingham Palace and asked if he would accept an MBE in the coming New Year's Honours. He asked me not to mention the MBE to anyone.

After a long and sometimes very difficult life it was clear that this delighted him. With an air of some sadness but also quiet resignation he said: 'How lovely to receive some public recognition at what must be the end of a career of more than fifty years' writing.'

We talked about the famous few lines that are quoted at the front of all his books – endless speculation and enquiry has not revealed where these lines come from, but BB insisted that his father had copied them from a north country tombstone. This may well be true, but whoever commissioned the headstone almost certainly knew the lines from Robert Browning's famous poem 'Fra Lippo Lippi' which in part at least echo the tombstone lines: Browning's life-loving monk almost shouts:

You've seen the world
The beauty and the wonder and the power,
The shapes of things, their colours, lights and shades,
Changes, surprises, – and God made it all!

Coincidence perhaps but the lines in BB's version do clearly sum up his view of life. We don't know if BB was eventually reconciled to a God his father would have understood but he did not attend church nor did he ever express a conventional Christian view of life and death and it is hard not to believe that he found it difficult to accept an afterlife that did not include the physical senses; the sense of touch, sight, smell and hearing – senses that make the wonder of the world accessible to human beings. He believed that the natural world was man's real home and that to be part of it meant enjoying every day in as close contact as possible with nature. The world of the spirit without the physical world – its colours lights and shades – was not worth having.

BB's earliest fear – and it is one with which *A Child Alone* begins – was that he would die because he knew that he was ill and might have to have a dangerous operation. The prospect of an operation was terrifying in the small child's mind, but when BB went into hospital in September 1990 he was no longer afraid as he had been almost a century earlier. He had been planning a trip to the Solway in search of geese and had even booked a day at a hospital in Glasgow where he could have his regular dialysis. But a sudden collapse meant the trip did not take place; he was taken to Northampton General Hospital and to the operating theatre. On 8 September he died while under the anaesthetic. It was as if the wheel had come full circle; his early fears, tempered now by a long life in the natural world he loved, had come to an end.

The image that haunted BB throughout his life was the vanished village at Faxton. He found it curiously moving that he should have been alive at a time when there was still a village so remote that no road or track went to it. He was moved too by the gradual abandonment of the village – the idea that a village could be abandoned will strike those born more recently than BB as astonishing. Most of us know about abandoned medieval villages but the fact that a village could still disappear in the early part of the twentieth century is remarkable.

Partly BB was moved by the fate of Faxton because it was the death of a rural community; the death and disappearance of an ancient village cut off from the world. But he was also moved by the idea that nature had once again taken over the

BB towards the end of his life.

lonely fields where the village had once stood and where now the visitor will find only a stone memorial to the medieval church where the Reverend Walter Watkins-Pitchford once preached and where his small son sat in an ancient pew and heard the birdsong distantly through the coloured glass.

BB believed that man was part of nature and that nature would be there long after man had gone and the saddest part of that was that man would no longer hear the birdsong, or smell the wet grass in spring or the autumn rain.

# INDEX